The Bard & Co

The Bard & Co

Shakespeare's role in modern business

Edited by Jim Davies, John Simmons & Rob Williams

CYANBOOKS

First published in 2007 by Cyan Books, an imprint of

Cyan Communications Limited
119 Wardour Street
London W1F 0UW
United Kingdom
T: +44 (0)20 7565 6120
E: sales@cyanbooks.com
www.cyanbooks.com

A CIP record for this book is available from the British Library

ISBN-13 978-1-905736-18-8
ISBN-10 1-905736-18-5

Typeset by Phoenix Photosetting, Lordswood, Chatham, Kent

Printed and bound in Great Britain by
Creative Print & Design Group (Wales), Ebbw Vale

The Names of the Principall Actors in all these Playes.

William Shakespeare.
Richard Burbadge.
John Hemmings.
Augustine Phillips.
William Kempt.
Thomas Poope.
George Bryan.
Henry Condell.
William Slye.
Richard Cowly.
John Lowine.
Samuell Crosse.
Alexander Cooke.

Samuel Gilburne.
Robert Armin.
William Ostler.
Nathan Field.
John Underwood.
Nicholas Tooley.
William Ecclestone.
Joseph Taylor.
Robert Benfield.
Robert Goughe.
Richard Robinson.
John Shancke.
John Rice.

Contents

Preface

Actors love seeing their names alongside the dramatis personae at the beginning of a published play. There is often a touching moment towards the end of rehearsals. Just as the production is moving out of the rehearsal room and into the theatre, the writer will receive the hot-off-the-press first run of printed copies. In a ritual act of generosity—which is always touching, no matter how regularly it happens—the author distributes a copy to each and every actor. They immediately flick to the cast list at the front, their eyes quick with paranoia that their name will be spelt wrong, and hungry for the confirmation that it is concretely there.

Of all artists, none has their work so completely written on water as the theatre actor. The permanence of actors' work on film and video has obscured from us the essential impermanence of their trade. A critic's words, the stories of spectators, old sketches and photographs can give us an idea of a performance, but it is no replacement for being there. This is one of the central joys of a theatre performance, that it is happening each time once and once only, that it is dying as fast as it is being created, and that once done it will disappear for ever. But it is also, when an actor is out of work or full of gripe, an occasional cause of sorrow. Actors, like all of us, want some recognition of the fact that they were there. The list of actors at the beginning of a play is a small weapon against oblivion.

No list of actors is as mysterious or as celebrated or as intriguing as the bunch of bandits who worked at the Globe in its first manifestation. We know little of who they were or what their performances were like, but we do know that they were performing under conditions that would make most of our actors blanch with terror, and that they also inspired a generation of writers to compose a body of work unparalleled in history for breadth, vivacity, wit and life. They must have been extraordinary beasts to cope with the level of distraction, riot and noise around them, and extraordinary artists to handle such delicate and fine switchbacks of thought and feeling. We know little of them, but we do, thanks to the First Folio, have a list of their names to stimulate our imaginations.

On the list—which happens to have 26 names on it—is William Shakespeare. He got luckier than the rest in terms of his contribution to posterity: he left behind a few plays that have had a not insignificant impact on the world ever since. We know how far these plays, and the verse within them, have reached into the world and into all of our lives. Novels, operas, ballets, films, landscapes, lives, relationships and goodness knows what else have all been profoundly inspired or influenced by Shakespeare's plays. This book is another example of this influence, demonstrating his continuing inspiration for people working and writing in the business world today. These 26 contemporary writers have been paired with a Shakespeare play and a member of the original company. And, given this common starting point, play plus player, they have each been briefed: make of it what you will. Each has put the play at the centre, and many but not all have shed new light through the reconstruction of the original actor's role.

I am sure that those actors, as complicated in their attitudes to posterity as any group of performers, would be tickled pink by the idea that, four centuries down the line, a group of writers would be attempting to capture some sense of their lives and their contribution to the world. That they would be so solidly remembered, even if sometimes, given a void of biographical information, imagination has had to work harder than memory. Will Shakespeare, on behalf of the company, might be the proudest of the lot because as a writer and theatre man he valued what these actors could do to give meaning and life to his words. As a sort of proxy custodian of their ghosts, I am delighted to pass on thanks and best wishes to this project.

Dominic Dromgoole
Artistic Director
Shakespeare's Globe

Introduction, or *What You Will*

John Simmons on the *Sonnets*

This book could change the way you do business. When you think of business, perhaps you think of a spreadsheet: the bottom line, the value added, the rationality of numbers. In the end it all comes down to profit and loss. Of course.

But business is about people, and therefore it's about emotion. It's about you and me deciding we'd rather buy from X than Y because X makes us feel better about ourselves. Which then has a knock-on effect on the bottom line. Of course.

When two business people get together, they rarely talk only in numbers. Businesses are less about numbers than about language.

There, I've said it. What an uncomfortable thought for any business. Not only do you have to make sure that your numbers add up to 100 per cent but your words have to achieve a similar completeness. Impossible, I admit. But what a stimulating challenge. A linguistic balance sheet, a verbal accounting: with William Shakespeare as the auditor.

The word is not lightly introduced. We need auditors of business language, and who better than Shakespeare to play that role? We need to listen. Oh the play that Shakespeare would have had with modern business words like audit and account, before even venturing into the obscure forests of synergy, leverage and metrics. The business world has mountains of abstract concepts, and we stand daunted in the valleys and foothills of empowerment, fearful to advance.

Shakespeare showed us that the pen is the way to advance. It was the means he used to further his own advancement, negotiating his way through the tortuous politics of his day, knowing that he was effectively the hired man of an important client, one of the King's Men. Ponder this thought as you read the first chapter in this book, Stuart Delves' telling of Shakespeare's diary on the eve of the first performance of *Macbeth*.

That chapter is the prologue to the stories that follow. There are 26 chapters by 26 writers who work in the business world; 26 because they are members of the organization 26 (a name derived from the number of letters in the alphabet). 26 aims to create greater understanding and respect for the role of words in our working life.

There is another reason for 26 chapters in this book. It came about originally when I was talking with Patrick Spottiswoode, Education Director of Shakespeare's Globe Theatre. Patrick in his disarmingly casual way produced Shakespeare's First Folio Plays and pointed to the list of "Principall Actors." The list, headed by Shakespeare himself, includes Burbage, Kemp and Hemmings plus relatively unknown actors and shareholders in the original Globe. There are 26 of them in all. There seemed to be at least a numerical connection across the centuries. Perhaps there would be other connections too?

So we teamed 26 contemporary writers for business with the members of Shakespeare's acting company. We allocated each writer a Shakespeare play as well as an original actor. Then we asked them to research, contemplate, explore, study and write. The inspiration for the writing was principally the play itself—the thing, as Hamlet described it—with the actor as an optional source of inspiration. We asked the writers to explore Shakespeare's relevance to modern business, with a particular focus on his language.

The writers were chosen, plays and players were randomly assigned. And work began. One of the writers said to me: "The sheer volume of material out there is debilitating." Shakespeare has become something of an industry. There's no doubt that Shakespeare represents the greatest challenge in our culture for any writer. Even those (some of them here) who don't actually *enjoy* Shakespeare still feel the need to acknowledge his supremacy. It's enough to make any of us curl up and mumble "pass."

But then a second reaction sets in. It is a challenge but the challenge is not to write as well as Shakespeare. Instead, it is to find something in an ancient work that touches us and illuminates us four centuries after its creation.

Shakespeare, as you will read, retains that power to connect with our humanity. As well as insights into Shakespeare's plays, and into the relevance of Shakespeare to our lives today, you will find here examples of imaginative writing, proof that he can still inspire creativity. Great writing remains the most powerful inspiration for a writer. We should read more. And we should read differently. Then perhaps we would write differently.

There have been other approaches to Shakespeare and business, often focusing on his ability to demonstrate leadership qualities to management. Consultants have drawn particularly on *Henry V* to explore what it means to be a leader in modern business, and *Hamlet* to point out the perils of indecision. This book, however, does not go into the role-model potential of Shakespeare's characters, enabling managers to step once more into the breach of poor results or to counter the slings and arrows of outrageous business fortune. Shakespeare's enduring relevance to us comes from his wielding of the power of words. Our conclusion is that language provides the best leadership. And in business, as in everyday life, we neglect this at our peril.

The writers here explore different aspects of this message. In doing so they cover most areas of business life, from issues like power, strategy, identity, persuasion, mergers and acquisitions to particular techniques like storytelling, presentation skills, workshops, the influence of environments, creative partnerships and the use of silence. They explore "spin," of course. They analyse shifting meanings of a word like "fortune" with its talismanic power in an entrepreneurial world. They carry out their explorations with seriousness and with wit, and there is much here to make you laugh as well as think. But they return to the theme of language because that defines them as professionals and informs their belief in themselves as writers influencing the business world. Above all, they take an intensely personal approach to their given play and their subject, because they believe in their own role as writers and the potential of language to change, improve and liberate.

Some of the writers have adopted their player wholeheartedly, others have ignored him completely. It was not a requirement. The use (or not) of the player might encourage readers to consider the nature of creativity. We all welcome creative stimulation but there is never a formula for it. Kemp, Eccleston, Burbage and others have provided inspiration beyond the grave in ways that would have surprised them.

The inspiration provided to me was neither play nor actor. I have been looking at Shakespeare and business through the lens of the *Sonnets*, a sequence of 154 poems written in a strict poetic form. The *Sonnets* are often quoted ("Shall I compare thee to a summer's day?") but little read. Should they be? And, if so, do they have any particular message for people in business today?

The *Sonnets* are not as most people imagine them. They are certainly not simple lyrics eulogizing a female lover. In fact, the *Sonnets* have been travestied since the time of their publication by what we now consider a completely modern form of marketing hype. Here, for example, is the way the publisher John Benson introduced them in the 1640 edition:

> *In your perusal you shall finde them seren, cleere and eligantly plaine, such gentle straines as shall recreate and not perplexe your braine, no intricate or cloudy stuffe to puzzell intellect, but perfect eloquence.*

This is in the tradition of salesmanship that believes it's better not to let the truth interfere with a strong selling message. The *Sonnets* serene, clear and plain? I think not. There's enough here to puzzle any intellect, and that is their great challenge. A reading of the complete sequence convinced me of this, and made me wonder how I might use the *Sonnets* with other business writers.

The sonnet is a good example of writing within formal constraints. There are strict limits on lines, rhymes, syllables, metre. Much of my work is training people to write more effectively and creatively for business—and I use formal constraints of various kinds to challenge people and to liberate them from business writing formulas. The more I became absorbed in the *Sonnets*, the more I became intrigued by the possibilities of using them to develop writing techniques in a business context. So I conducted an experiment.

In September 2006 I ran a five-day writing course in Spain, taking a group of business writers to a remote villa in Aracena. This "Dark Angels" course was designed as creative refreshment for the group. I asked each participant to read one sonnet (No. 138) in advance. This is a sonnet about deception and self-deception, and its closing couplet brings this theme home with multiple meanings and a breathtaking rightness.

Therefore I lie with her, and she with me,
And in our faults by lies we flattered be.

Put this with other examples of final couplets, and the rich playfulness of Shakespeare's language defies easy explanation but encourages contemplation.

In all external grace you have some part
But you like none, none you, for constant heart. (No. 53)

His beauty shall in these black lines be seen,
And they shall live, and he in them still green. (No. 63)

In Aracena, I set the group one exercise designed to explore:

- the intellectual puzzle of reading sonnets
- the use of metaphor to illuminate and reinforce a theme
- the ability to use apt words to create a satisfying ending
- the role of sound to guide writing and understanding.

I was interested too in the different way in which you *read* a sonnet. It is a form of reading unlike reading a novel, newspaper or annual report. It demands attention. It's closer to the way we need to read to edit our own writing.

I have no doubt that while at work or in the office we spend too little time with our brains engaged. We skim over the surface of problems, immediately seeking to apply previously tried solutions to them. A business can keep chugging along as a result but it seldom allows flashes of real illumination or inspiration to enter its intellectual life. Indeed most businesses would shy away from the very suggestion of having an intellectual life. There is almost a pride in the elevation of action over thought. *Just do it* is probably the world's most admired and adopted strap line. Better to do something than think something.

A heretical alternative, encouraged by Shakespeare, is that it's better to act as a result of thinking that goes beyond the formulaic. But how can we achieve that kind of thinking if we have completely lost the habit of intellectual pursuit for its own excitement? Our business activities are obsessed by the need to reach numbers and targets, as if the abstract notions of percentages or volumes are ideas that in themselves yield revelations. The difference between +5 per cent or –5 per cent is the difference between success or failure in business (a Micawberish notion), but what gives you the ability to achieve success is the application of thought, as well as those modern imperatives of business behaviour such as commitment, passion, drive and energy. Such values are useless without thought to direct the way they are used.

I circulated Sonnet 138 in advance. It had all the attributes of a Shakespearean sonnet: intellectual playfulness, technical linguistic dexterity, verbal ambiguity and the absolute rejection of words as pure, straightforward and devoid of alternative interpretations. If nothing else, Shakespeare tells us "nothing is, or need be, as it first seems." There is always a subtext, there is always the potential for other meanings, other explanations. We all play games with honesty and integrity. Welcome to the world. Welcome to the world of business.

When my love swears that she is made of truth,
I do believe her, though I know she lies,
That she might think me some untutored youth
Unlearned in the world's false subtleties.
Thus vainly thinking that she thinks me young,
Although she knows my days are past the best,
Simply I credit her false-speaking tongue;
On both sides thus is simple truth suppressed.
But wherefore says she not she is unjust?
And wherefore say not I that I am old?
O love's best habit is in seeming trust,
And age in love loves not t' have years told:
Therefore I lie with her, and she with me,
And in our faults by lies we flattered be.

The sonnet plays with the meaning of meaning. It nudges and winks to a bewildering degree. It takes the word "lie" as the focus of its attention, then comes to terms with the word by getting into bed with it. In that sense, it could be seen as shocking. But Shakespeare is never a straightforward companion.

Having accustomed people (I hoped) to the form, texture and sound of a sonnet, I then introduced another exercise into the process. I gave each participant a copy of Sonnet 97, but stripped it of its final couplet.

How like a winter hath my absence been
From thee, the pleasure of the fleeting year!
What freezings have I felt, what dark days seen,
What old December's bareness everywhere!
And yet this time removed was summer's time,
The teeming autumn big with rich increase
Bearing the wanton burden of the prime,
Like widowed wombs after their lords' decease:
Yet this abundant issue seemed to me
But hope of orphans, and unfathered fruit;
For summer and his pleasures wait on thee,
And thou away, the very birds are mute;

I then asked people to write a final couplet to complete the sonnet. Try it yourself. This is tough. There is no easy sonnet. No sonnet yields itself to prose translation, so even teasing out the meaning is difficult. With each sonnet we have to find an individual interpretation. Earlier in the week at Aracena we had asked this group of native English speakers to "translate" a page from *Don Quixote*. Cervantes, in seventeenth-century Spanish, was in many ways an easier challenge than Shakespeare with his seventeenth-century English but geological layers of meaning.

We read Sonnet 97, exploring its metaphorical complexities. We read it and we listened; listening became a vital part of the process. The sound of language contains the essence of its meaning. Like the result of the distillation process, what you have at the end is the pure essence of the thing itself. If we can only understand and analyse it.

The more I have written for business, the more I have trained people to write for business, the more I am convinced of the primacy of sound. In workshops the absolute essential is the spoken performance of words written. Respond in writing to an exercise, a constraint, then read it out to the group who have been set the same challenge. The learning comes from doing, then listening. It always works. And there is no better ally in this than Shakespeare, whose words sing, soar, persuade, inveigle, entice, challenge and even antagonize. Better any reaction than no reaction. Corporate leaders, listen to me. And listen to yourselves.

What provokes a reaction is not just language and the technicalities of language—there is no escaping the formal difficulties of rhyme, metre and archaisms—but the certainty of belief in metaphor. Without metaphor sonnets do not exist. Often the metaphorical reference is simple. Much revolves around nature and the seasons. This is universal stuff but it also has the advantage that what worked in 1607 still works in 2007. In business writing we tend to shun metaphor, but much of my own teaching and writing aims to restore it to a central role in the national theatre of business. Our managerial writing has been stripped of drama, colour and imagery because it has been denied metaphor. Let's make it once again the town centre, the hub of activities, the place from which we spring off in all directions in search of life, meaning and everything.

The aim, in setting the exercise of "completing the sonnet," was not to outdo Shakespeare. Many people will think there is something almost sacrilegious in the attempt to do such an exercise. I share some of that feeling but I also believe Shakespeare is bigger than any such petty considerations. He might have dismissed the outcomes ("not good enough") but he would not have scorned the effort ("let's try it"). In a sense, it would have mirrored his own practice. While accepting his genius and while being in awe of it, I also believe he would have produced many alternative versions of a sonnet before committing it to publication.

In that spirit, here are some of the versions produced in the workshop.

When with thee once again I greet the spring,
Then shall those voiceless birds begin to sing.

Susannah

Thus pregnant with the seasons will our partings be
And we, expecting less, the more their labours see.

Philip

And if our seasons still stay unaligned
My summer too stays wintrily maligned.

Neil

All seasons pass, each year its end must find,
For darkened hearts to brighten and lives together bind.

John M

So summer and winter become as one,
Awaiting your touch, until undone.

Iain

And though in real'ty it still winter be,
What clouds will fade when you return to me.

Lorelei

None of them is as good as the real Shakespeare:

Or if they sing, 'tis with so dull a cheer
That leaves look pale, dreading the winter's near.

The point was not to improve but to explore. We can all explore in order to improve—not to improve Shakespeare but to improve our own writing by better understanding the nature of language. And by tuning our ears to the rightness of individual words. What happens is that each writer brings the sonnet's theme to an apt conclusion, a useful technique for any business communicator and a vital thought process for anyone working in an organization. I can see only benefits from using Shakespeare as an exemplar to improve the quality of thinking and writing at work.

Nothing spurs us on as much as competition. Nothing inspires a writer as much as another writer. It's the whole basis for clients going out to a "competitive pitch." *Go on, show me*. What if we take Shakespeare as the competitor? Come on, A, B, D & C, you say you are the world's most inspiring ad agency, but imagine that you're up against a copywriter called William Shakespeare. Come on,

AnyBrand, you say your brand values are passion, drama, empathy and honesty—but now you're up against your greatest competitor, The Bard & Co. How will you rise to that challenge?

Perhaps that is the greatest gauntlet this book throws down. It's simply a challenge to strive not just for the good, but for the hand-on-heart, bow-down, kiss-the-earth superlative of "we want to do something that has never been done before so well." There is simply too much mediocre work about and too many companies prepared to aspire only to the acceptable.

Challenge yourself. Use Shakespeare as the ultimate challenge.

In the business context, when I use the word "writer" don't think too narrowly. I mean anyone who uses words at work. You might be the logistics expert, the marketing manager, the chief executive, the financial director, the independent chairman, the HR specialist, the commercial consultant. You all use words. Words are your opportunity to gain power. Seize them, seize it.

What Shakespeare shows us is simply this. Language is everything. Ignore it and you're lost. You cannot operate as a business without a deep understanding of the power of words and their potential to change our attitudes, our hearts and our behaviour. You cannot get your business right until you get its words right.

One Read

Stuart Delves on *Macbeth*

Principal Actor: William Shakespeare

Dearest Chuck

When last I stole away from your side I could not sleep. It has been thus for many a night over many a week. I have drunk a firkin of wine; prayed; wept for sleep. My mind has burned long after the snuffed candle's smoke wisps away. Images of horror have assailed me, so real I swear I catch the scent of them. And like a swaddled child, a small boat in a big bed, every timber's creak has heralded the hangman of doom. I've seen his hands so oft I can trace the weals. But tonight I feel some respite or, at least, the abeyance of din and the aversion of the spectre's glassy eye.

The play is done. Written more in blood and pitch than even Lear. It opens in an hour or so here at Hampton Court: under an August moon. (What harvest it will bear, I know not.) Of course it's played the Globe and seen stout wives ushered out as white as linen, but there's little politics there. I play a porter. Only this once, for Armin is sickening—but will be well again soon enough. (Poor Bob, I cram darkness in his jests as a chamberlain crams tobacco in a pipe. The Fool was his star turn; this sentinel a damned, lonely spot.) But it's a suitable role to undertake before the King. For indeed, in this play, I open the gate to hell.

And in hell I've been, my love. Not only in that I've inhabited the robes of a killer and his miss—and found the patterns of their cloth upon mine own flesh—but that I too must scotch something dear to me, as close as breath. Do you follow (portents are often hidden in the beguilement of a familiar smile)? Follow not, too soon. In earnest I want you to know a little of the journey I've taken in order to better understand the path that lies in front. You guess.

Maybe a letter is already writ in your own script, sealed and final, released and in the instructed hand of a servant? And yet I falter. Maybe it is best you be innocent of the knowledge. You see my indecision upon the page! And my resolve. You shall be privy to my briary path. Even though this letter will, I do not doubt, be one read then consigned to the flames. Indeed, maybe with this, all my loose and tender words will turn to the senile green of daylight embers.

Be that as it may. I am the King's man: that you know and understand. I too play the courtier in that the business of writing is to please and to please most the One upon whom one's livelihood depends. There are those who have o'er stepped these bounds and, rightly or wrongly, not cloaked their blades within their craft. Tom hung. Kit stabbed. Ben branded. I have laundered my survival—inseparable from royal indulgence—late by the candle's tallow: checking my heart against my head; cooling the furnace to the flare of a courtyard brazier where all may warm their hands not burn them.

But it pleases me well that our King is learned and that his thoughts brood on those dark spirits that stalk the twilight, beckon and decoy. Some, like Bacon, would dismiss such sightings as I've penned as fancy or phantasms and say, "Look, in the light of reason they vanish!" And Bacon is a wiser man than me. Wiser even than the Wisest Fool. But this I know, power is cast on the devil's anvil. All who would grasp its rings beware. And the necessary drive? It is fed by signs and messages that rasp our every sense and feed upon our vanity.

The subject is too sprawling for a letter, too facetted for a sonnet. The drama will play it out for, as in life, it's by our actions that we are blessed or damned. How oft a Lord's public honours, a general's admiration from his men conceals an agony of mind that preys upon a conscience that cannot shun the knowledge of what the hand has done? Words on paper, dagger in heart—both are weighed in the same scale. In this "Macbeth" I have the usual cast of lords and ladies to tell a tale of vaulting ambition and its fatal consequences. The hero is a thornier, wider, darker, more brilliant Brutus. But unlike Caesar, the play is not titled "King Duncan."

I sail close to the wracking wind. But this creation dwarfs all others upon the stage excepting only his wife and lady. They are as close as armour to naked shoulder blade, the outer and inner of one, in an unravelling dance of darkness. And most potently, and here diplomacy plays trumps into my hand, I bring out from the wings the wyrds themselves. They appear in the form of witches, ancient and ghastly to behold but they hold aloft the glass of destiny. What man of spunk would not cleave a thicket, a copse, a forest to look into it? But no man, then or now, can read it straight. For every sign and picture that it conjures twists and curves in equivocation.

Not since Richard, Duke of Gloucester, have I breathed life into so black a being. But Macbeth does not possess a heart so black. He is altogether greater than the dazzling hunchback, for though he shares his lust for power he lacks his hideous charm. Shows instead the face behind. Not since Hamlet have I turned a part so inward. My jewel, you do not know the recent desert of my soul, more scorched than the Saharan sands. You say you do. You've chided me for my silences. You've sought to bring me cheer. You've seen a gloom maybe but you have not seen its blind black origin. Methinks I mask it well but it's in my work. Lover, husband, friend, father (how fitting that that tails the list: it stings, believe me)—these are roles by which we play with each other, whether as cat with mouse or mares wild upon the heath. We play for real. But in our work are the workings of the mind, the shadow of the soul. (How abject it is then, when in a man's life his work is menial, stripped of imagination. And what priceless gift our theatre.) In Lear I kissed the very dust of the pit. I voyaged into nothing. In that great absence of hope my soul was paralysed. But here, with Macbeth, in the very pincer of fate, the welled strength of the man returns. He reaches again to the coil within, his will. When Fate has played its last twisted trick on him, jeering at the false certainties he has built, he cries out:

I will not yield
To kiss the ground before young Malcolm's feet,
And to be baited with the rabble's curse.
Though Birnam wood be come to Dunsinane,
And thou opposed, being of no woman born,
Yet I will try the last. Before my body
I throw my warlike shield: lay on Macduff;
And damned be him that first cries "Hold, enough!"

Will. Ha! Of occasion I have sought out this apothecary, a man selling tinctures and herbs from a casement at Ludgate. He knows me. He makes a good potion for settling the nerves. Many of us go to him. One day he took me aside and I do not know if flattery was his purpose and what he hoped for in reward, but he told me that dukes of ancient magic, from Merlin to those today who shall not be named, say that man is made of will. And he bade me look. Taking a gnarled stick of charcoal he drew upon a napkin of cloth thus—with the W for arms, the stem of the I for the body, the dot for the head and the two Ls for legs:

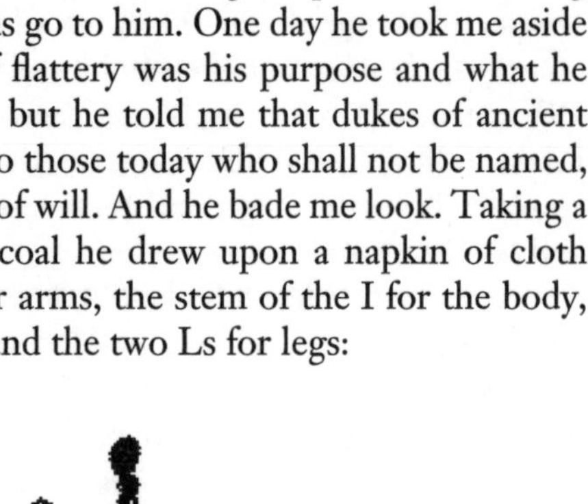

It pleased me and dwells with me yet. Will is in Macbeth. And Macbeth in Will perchance. But who was this thane who would be king? By way of late conversation, I learnt from the King's Recorder—a sage steeped in the lore of his warrior kingdom and making show of it here in London—that Macbeth in the Gaelic tongue means "Son of Life." Forsooth his deeds, by this Scots account, contrast with Holinshed's. But Macbeth's line is scrunched in a child's tomb on some holy skerry in a ferocious sea. The Stuart line is my concern. In the politics of the play at least. And it is too distant a history for even James to take great heed of. But my greater concern is with the globe within, where all life's threads tangle in their fateful weave. Drayton quipped that my Macbeth is more like the son of death. But no. The fruit of life is raw potential and just as nature swings from storm to June dew, so we must make what we will of that nature which is ours.

And his wife? She had a name. And divine right to the crown as well. But I deny her a name. And give her avarice's brooding halo. She steps forth as Lady. He addresses her with endearment as is the wont of lovers. Like us, they are two halves of one soul. She is the clearer and fiercer but the one whose reason is ransacked by guilt. She breaks. He is more soft to impression and sorely troubled yet, when hounded, calls on his soldier's nerves and holds fast: defies fate: strides into final battle every inch a king.

The ecstasy in this dual writing I cannot describe. I have dragged my face with her nails. Not only that. I have stolen your perfume, smelt your blood. You must think me mad, greatly affected. Much of this will make little sense until you hear the play. Watch for the chamber scene of disarray and piteous tears, when she, too, cannot sleep. You will go? Sit centre. (Have your maid call by and I will assure this.) Listen to the flint in Burbage's speech. It has all the unvanquished crag of Scotland that gives this man his mettle.

You will not think me a man of mettle. You will think me a coward, lily livered. But I was crueller to Cordelia than Holinshed. As cruel as nature was to my Hamnet; to Lady Macbeth's offspring. And I must be cruel, to thee. To us.

Life's but a walking shadow, a poor player
That struts and frets his hour upon the stage,
And then is heard no more: it is a tale
Told by an idiot, full of sound and fury
Signifying nothing.

I wrote these lines. Will hear them in an hour's time. In another man's mouth. A man playing the part of another. But they are mine. Hear my voice in them.

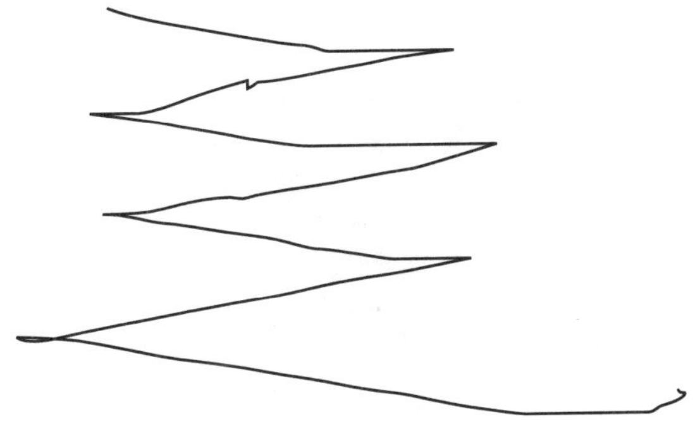

How poetry deserts me when I have most need of it! How would I have disentangled Romeo from Juliet or Juliet from Romeo? If tragedy had not befallen them and their houses had opened their shutters to each other's? If they had moved beyond the first flushes of love? How *then*, my Sheba, when Solomon's song had lost its ring? How would I have parted Orlando and Rosalind? A closer match to ours, my Alexandrian.

My thoughts dwell more and more on Stratford. There I have a wife and daughters—daughters who know me not as roundly as they should. There I have a house, mine own house with barns, beasts and grain: wealth, arms, status—all that should bless age; the riches and rewards of careful schemes. And with the passing of our Golden Age, London holds little for me, but you. And you, you must enjoy the pride of your years as I must learn to speak true and with nonpareil in praise of another's veined ripeness. In short, I must return more often to my Anne's bed. There, I've writ it. The other is yours to keep and even though I writhe in scratching this, I expect not that you keep it warm for me. I must not come to you again. Must strangle all thought of it.

I know our names and reputations are safe in each other's hands (you and I picked each other tellingly, keen to both thorn and petal) but in your own heart, I pray, have no mercy on me. Spit and blast, my Rosamund, rose of my world. For my part, I will ache for you. I will not sleep. Will write for you still, the singing lines that are my heart's alone. And yes, like a vain fool, I would have you remember me at my unguarded, private, bawdy best: when all the world but you and I was beyond the curtain.

Curse me.

Will Shakespeare

The Player: A Presentation Masterclass with Richard Burbage

Dan Radley on *Antony and Cleopatra*

Principal Actor: Richard Burbage

Every performer knows the feeling: you have something important to say, but when it comes to standing in front of the people whose approval you seek, you die a miserable death.

Remember the first time you shuffled on stage as a trembling infant in the school nativity to announce the miracle of a star rising in the east and, lo, promptly wet yourself? Remember how you vowed never to appear on stage again?

And now look at you, burbling away in front of a PowerPoint slide—powerless and pointless. You're like that non-Welsh-speaking Welsh Secretary rum-ti-tumming along to *Mae Hen Wlad Fy Nhadau*. If you think the audience hasn't noticed, you're mistaken. They always notice.

For four hundred years, I've enjoyed my fair share of critical acclaim: "A delightful Proteus so wholly transforming himself into his Part, and putting off himself with his Cloathes, as he never, not so much as in the Tyringhouse, assum'd himself again until the play was done." Oh, you're too kind.

I was Shakespeare's original Lear in *King Lear*, Macbeth in *Macbeth*, Hamlet in *Hamlet*. And yet I recall with a shudder my uncertain opening night as Antony at the Globe. Having failed to raise a laugh with my bungled suicide and the immortal line, "Not dead? Not dead?" one of the bearpit shouted out, "Yes, dead."

The fact is, most great work is rejected because it's presented badly—hence today's masterclass. I shall be sharing performance techniques developed with my good friend Will and exploring *The Tragedy of Antony and Cleopatra*, a play that often triumphantly fails to live up to its reputation in performance. To assist me, Jackie Kane will be playing the part of Cleopatra.

Jackie, I want you to imagine you're preparing for a four-hour meeting with the three most powerful men in the western world. No pressure, but they've brought with them a sycophantic entourage of soothsayers, soldiers and servants, plus three thousand observers who, secretly, would rather be at home watching *Desperate Housewives*.

First piece of advice: don't rely on theatricality. There's more to Cleopatra than her appetite for self-dramatization. "Age cannot wither her," wrote Will, "nor custom stale her infinite variety." So being actressy won't be enough. You need to *be* Cleopatra.

Let's pick it up in Act 5, Scene 2. Cleopatra has been taken captive by Proculeius and is threatening to starve herself. Jackie, I want you to voice this in a whisper. Make it interior. Convince yourself you really mean it.

[JK] *Sir, I will eat no meat. I'll not drink, sir.*
If idle talk will once be necessary,
I'll not sleep neither. This mortal house I'll ruin,
Do Caesar what he can.

They're planning to humiliate you in front of the crowds in Rome—how do you feel about that?

[JK] *Rather a ditch in Egypt*
Be gentle grave unto me; rather on Nilus' mud
Lay me stark naked, and let the waterflies
Blow me into abhorring; rather make
My country's high pyramides my gibbet,
And hang me up in chains.

Really shock yourself with your conviction. You're The Player now.

Back in '67, I played opposite Zoe Caldwell—now there's a committed actress!—who hennaed the palms of her hands to *feel* more Egyptian. Zoe's dressing room became a shrine to eastern eroticism, and there she would mix perfumed oils into her makeup until she was fragrant from head to foot. Before each performance, she'd urge me to "Take up the male oxygen!" I had no idea what she meant, but I was smitten.

Let's return to the boardroom for a moment. However passionately you believe in your presentation, it's worth remembering the audience is principally there to spoil it. Their agenda runs like this: Item 1.1 Disregard, unsettle and interrupt; 1.2 Answer mobile phone (eventually) after polyphonic rendition of *Crazy Frog*; 1.3 Munch, snooze and generally show off to one another.

If you want them to tune in to you, start fast. The first 90 seconds set the tone. Jackie, can we take it from the top? Act 1, Scene 1…

[JK] *If it be love indeed, tell me how much.*

Cleopatra's opening line is a burnished hand-grenade of beaten gold. The kind of innocuous remark every man dreads—how much do you love me? As Antony flounders, Cleo teases him about the hold that Caesar and Antony's wife Fulvia have over him.

[JK] *Do this, or this;*
Take in that kingdom, and enfranchise that.
Perform't, or else we damn thee.

Now go for the jugular …

[JK] *As I am Egypt's Queen,*
Thou blushest, Antony, and that blood of thine
Is Caesar's homager; else so thy cheek pays shame
When shrill-tongued Fulvia scolds. The
messengers!

Under pressure, Antony launches a romantic counter-offensive. Like this …

[RB] *Let Rome in Tiber melt, and the wide arch*
Of the ranged empire fall! Here is my space.
Kingdoms are clay. Our dungy earth alike
Feeds beast as man. The nobleness of life
Is to do thus—

Political duty has been tossed aside for personal gratification: they kiss!

[RB] *when such a mutual pair*
And such a twain can do't, in which I bind,
On pain of punishment, the world to weet
We stand up peerless.

[JK] *Excellent falsehood!*

Cleopatra bursts Antony's bubble with some rhetoric of her own. She's enjoyed the flattery but isn't buying any of it.

By this point, the audience has had its fill of culture. In my experience, what begins with a few stifled coughs of dissatisfaction can rapidly turn into a mass stampede for the exit. When Tallulah Bankhead played Cleopatra, one reviewer summed up the experience in a single sentence: "Last night she barged down the Nile and sank."

It's an awful feeling, but rejection must never undermine your confidence as a presenter. For The Player, redemption is only ever a performance away. Back in the days of *The King's Men*, the drama lived in our heads, and if the audience refused to laugh at a joke we changed it, scribbling and thribbling our way to the next performance.

How Will would have loved working with Dame Peggy—she had such an appetite for rehearsal. I remember one morning we'd been called in for Act 4, Scene 15. While the cast were still nursing their hangovers, Peggy slipped off her shoes, moved to the centre of the rehearsal space and launched into the same passage, over and over again, sketching her character like a frenzied miniaturist; her brush a blur of agitated daubs, exquisite strokes and iridescent outbursts.

Peggy had become fascinated by the ambiguities in Will's phrase, "the soldier's pole." Did he mean the Pole Star? A maypole? An erect penis? Or was he saying there were no more soldiers, only children to hold the flag? We watched spellbound as Peggy used each meaning to explore the colours of Cleopatra's personality. The first time she played the passage to the stars; then with military formality; then she danced it; then in a state of fevered fury; and finally, as if she was in spiritual free-fall …

[JK] *The crown o'th'earth doth melt. My lord!*
O, withered is the garland of the war,
The soldier's pole is fall'n; young boys and girls
Are level now with men; the odds is gone,
And there is nothing left remarkable
Beneath the visiting moon.

The rehearsal space fell silent. At one point a stage-hand dropped a metal clamp and the entire cast swung fiercely around to "shush!" him. With the gravity of the word "moon" still hanging in the air, Peggy slipped on her heels and clicked away, leaving the sadness behind her.

The irony is, Kenneth Tynan savaged her opening-night performance: "The great sluts of world drama lie beyond the ken of British actresses," wrote the critic. "An English Cleopatra is a contradiction in terms." Well, I have news for you, Ken. Some of my best friends are sluts, including several Dames of the British Empire.

Dame Judi, for example, may not have seemed an obvious choice as the serpent of old Nile. Indeed, an actor friend of mine once remarked that "she has a nice sense of comedy, but I can hear the background noise of hockey sticks bullying off." When we teamed up at the National, Judi even voiced doubts of her own to Sir Peter: "I hope you know what you're doing casting Cleopatra as a menopausal dwarf."

Once on stage, however, I found her outrageously sexy and convincing, playing Cleopatra at pace with unpredictable, snake-like head movements. For my part, I rough-and-tumbled her around the stage, as any battle-hardened Roman soldier would. For weeks we were black and blue as we improvised the love scenes in performance.

Here I should issue a note of caution: a highly charged, physical performance is unlikely to help you find favour in front of your assembled shareholders at the next AGM. I once played opposite an Enobarbus whose gestures were so mesmerizing, I'd defy any audience to follow what he was saying:

[RB] *O sovereign mistress of true melancholy*, [wipes away tear]
The poisonous damp of night disponge upon me, [wrings out an imaginary sponge]
di-BLAH di-BLAH di-BLAH di-BLAH di-BLAH,
May hang no longer on me. [Extends arms outwards, messiah-like, then clutches towards heart and throws outwards from chest into the audience.] *Throw my heart*
Against the flint and hardness of my fault, [stamps foot]
Which, being dried with grief, will break to powder, [grasps imaginary rock and crushes]

The whole speech was further blighted by a nasty case of irritable vowel syndrome that strangled all emotion. The best advice here is concentrate on speaking clearly and, if necessary, get someone to sew your cuffs together behind your back and tie your shoelaces together.

Disregard everything I've said so far: the essence of presentation is telling your side of the story in a brisk, clear voice. This is often all it takes to rest your case. Set the iambic metronome in your head to *allegro ma non troppo*, then project each pentameter with a great big rhythmical lungful.

There's no need to boom. Sometimes speaking with a deliberate hush forces the audience to lean forward attentively. Even at the Globe, with its open-air acoustics, I learnt to work the audience. The groundlings became my conduit, releasing the compressed energy of Will's verse with their laughter and lifting it up to the gods.

The critics raved: "Burbage doth not strive to make nature monstrous, she is often seen in the same scene as his but neither on stilts nor crutches. What we see him personate, we think truly done before us."

How did I fool them? Well, if you're playing Antony

and wish to appear naturalistic, my tip is always to make a move on Cleopatra. You owe it to the role to be romantically convincing, and there's a perfect opportunity in Act 4, Scene 4:

[RB] *Fare thee well, dame, whate'ere becomes of me:*
This is a soldier's kiss

So what kind of kiss can you get away with? Personally, I'd avoid the suction bear-hug with wobbly head action, pioneered recently by Nicholas Jones as Antony. If people really kissed like this the survival of the species would be in jeopardy.

Rather than pressing yourself upon Cleo on opening night—particularly if she despises you—keep the kisses light and imply eroticism to the audience through gentle caresses. The ideal time to reveal the extent of your amorous intentions is about a fortnight into the run when she's off guard. I've found the element of surprise will charge the production with a fresh burst of electricity. Whether Cleo reciprocates or not, apologize profusely backstage, explaining artistic experimentation as your motive. Remember, she has control of the winch in the final act and can leave you suspended indefinitely from her monument, like a carcass on a butcher's hook. What's more, she's probably knocking off Mardian the Eunuch, who's liable to punch your lights out in the wings.

If you're playing Cleopatra, you'll not only have randy Tony to contend with but also the challenge of the asp. Give us the line please, Jackie.

[JK] *Dost thou not see my baby at my breast,*
That sucks the nurse asleep?

You'll need to decide whether it's Cleopatra-like to expose the bits you're coaxing the snake to bite. The modern precedent was set over a century ago when Cora Brown-Potter first bared a breast. Frankie Barber, my most recent leading lady, judged it about right, I thought. She wore a semi-transparent robe that struck a balance between exhibitionism and regal dignity.

My very first Cleopatra was rather flat-chested, on

account of being a boy. So it was some compensation when I eventually played opposite Dame Helen, a wonderfully desirable queen. As I recall, she stood briefly naked before surrendering herself to "the joy of the worm."

Sad to report, there have been some misjudgements in this department. One RSC actress of advancing years flung off her golden robe in an ostentatious display of full-frontal nudity. Despite her infinite variety, age had withered her a little.

That's not naturalism, that's naturism. For me, the play's most vivid imagery is *spoken* in the stillness of an empty stage in Act 5, Scene 2. As Janet Suzman once said to me, "The impression of power in reserve is the single most riveting quality in a performer." And that's how I want you to play this. Let the verse paint Antony in a new light …

[JK] *His legs bestrid the ocean; his reared arm*
Crested the world; his voice was propertied
As all the tunèd spheres, and that to friends;
But when he meant to quail and shake the orb,
He was as rattling thunder. For his bounty,
There was no winter in't; an Antony it was
That grew the more by reaping.

Cleopatra builds layer upon layer of metaphor as she eulogizes Antony. He's the harmonious sound of planetary motion, a perpetual harvest, an arching dolphin …

[JK] *His delights*
Were dolphin-like; they showed his back above
The element they lived in. In his livery
Walked crowns and crownets; realms and island were
As plates dropped from his pocket.

The sensuality of the imagery provides a fitting climax to the drama and, with any luck, the audience leaves the theatre exhilarated.

Back in my day, theatregoers spoke of going to *hear* a play. Since then, I've seen amazing changes in the art of presentation. Oscar winners with just the one facial expression. Followers of Stanislavski who decline a television costume drama because it's not "proper acting," and yet can somehow be enticed out of bed for the massive royalties that accompany a voiceover for Cillit Bang. Still, my advice to The Player remains the same: let language create the spectacle.

If you ever die a death in front of an audience again, I want to be sure it's one of those glorious prolonged ones with a sword in your chest—or, rather, under your armpit—or with a trained, and preferably refrigerated, stage snake nibbling at a regally exposed titty.

Most of all, though, I want you to ditch the PowerPoint and seduce them by the ears.

Die each night, live for ever.

EXIT BURBAGE.

A Piperade and Peter: Marriage as Merger

Ezri Carlebach on *The Taming of the Shrew*

Principal Actor: John Hemmings

I stand somewhere on the South Bank of the Thames, licking a lolly. It's a hot day. I mustn't stain my top with lolly drips as I have a lunch date, and want to look good. Around and by me go the cheery tourists and weary locals. Below me, the Thames at low tide reveals a sludgy and unwelcoming beach. Gulls peck flotsam. A pigeon abruptly rolls over just at the water's edge, sending out an arc of Thamesdrops from her wingtips. So, that's how pigeons wash.

A preference for the hard path over the easy ride, for the strong taste over sweet nothings, is the tale told in *The Taming of the Shrew*. Fair Bianca, the younger of wealthy Baptista's daughters, cannot be married before her older sister Katherina. While Bianca appears meek and agreeable, Katherina is a "shrew"—strong-willed, proud and intelligent, and yet to encounter a man who she deems to be a match for her own sharp wit and steely spirit. Bianca's various suitors must, therefore, first find a husband for Katherina, someone who would woo a woman "curst and shrewd." Enter Petruchio, a man with a clear ambition:

I come to wive it wealthily in Padua;
If wealthily, then happily in Padua.[1]

He is quickly brought to Katherina's door and, inspired both by her father's dowry and by her beauty, Petruchio declares himself willing to tackle the challenge. In their early encounters, their "wooing" is full of word-play that is sufficiently ambiguous to allow for a range of motives on either part. But soon Petruchio boldly sets out his objective:

Thus in plain terms—your father hath consented
That you shall be my wife; your dowry 'greed on
And will you, nill you, I will marry you.[2]

He announces that they will wed the coming Sunday, and despite Katherina's retort that she'd sooner see him hanged, Baptista agrees to the deal. In the ensuing discussion the matter is cast in business terms, with Katherina a "commodity" that "lay fretting by," one from which Baptista seeks to make a gain. Petruchio is thus "a model for today's corporate executive who must initiate, guide, and deal with change,"[3] who approaches his goal of "wiving it wealthily" armed with "an audacious restructuring plan" for the unproductive asset that is Katherina.

Two men stop and lean on the railings above the river. I note sharp suits, slick hair, expensive shades. A sticky lolly rivulet trickles down my wrist and, swearing, I ditch the stick and search for a tissue. The suits are oblivious to my struggle, and as I dab I tune in to their talk.

"*... thinks we need an outside clean-team to handle sensitive data.*"
"*What does Will think?*"

---

1 *The Taming of the Shrew*, Act 1, Scene 2, 74–75.
2 *The Taming of the Shrew*, Act 2, Scene 1, 261–262.
3 Augustine, N. and Adelman, K. (1999) *Shakespeare in Charge: The Bard's Guide to Leading and Succeeding on the Business Stage*, New York: Hyperion Books.

"Will's not on board with this. He says the deal isn't close enough yet for us to consider that."
"What's your view?"
"Will's right. The market won't respond well to that kind of talk, it's premature. Will says ..."

I tune out again.

A merger occurs when two companies agree to become one. Frequently positioned as equals, most merger participants are not.[4] One usually has a dominant role and controls or tames, if you like, the other. Often there is a ritualistic mating dance between two parties prior to a deal that looks a lot like a somewhat prickly relationship taking shape, perhaps between two feisty lovers. Even in the relatively staid business press, the dominant metaphor used when describing prospective mergers is marriage. For instance, a merger is not an event but the beginning of a longer process, in the same way that a marriage is not just about the wedding. "Pre-merger talks are similar to dating, full of excitement and expensive dinners. The merger itself, or the wedding, is a formal ceremony full of promise.... There's a honeymoon period, then all hell breaks loose."[5] But pre-merger talks and pre-marriage banter aren't always like dating. They can be more like sparring, jostling for position, racking up a creative tension on which the respondents thrive. Early merger and acquisition talks can pose tricky questions: "Who would get what value from a deal? Who would govern the new entity? What legal boundaries must prospective partners be careful not to cross?"[6] Staking out the territory on these issues prior to the merger can appear more difficult than going down the "dating" route, but can provide for a stronger, more flexible relationship in the future. Might it be better if all hell breaks loose before the deal is done?

---

4 www.investopedia.com/university/mergers.

5 Thomas Atchinson, quoted in Conklin, M. (1994) Paying attention to basics can make or break a merger, *Health Care Strategic Management*, August, HCPro Inc.

6 De Smedt, S., Tortorici, V. & van Ockenburg, E. (2005) Reducing the risks of early M&A discussions, *Perspectives on Corporate Finance and Strategy*, Autumn, McKinsey & Company.

Clutching my now damp tissue, I wonder if the guys in the suits ever get sticky lolly juice up their sleeve just before an important meeting.

SHARP SUIT A (let's call him Peter) indicating sharp suit B: This is my colleague Curtis, from operations.

Curtis shakes hands with me.

ME: You have a damp, sticky tissue in your hand.
CURTIS: Yes, I just got lolly juice up my sleeve.
ME: I think we need an outside clean-team on this …

The success or failure of a particular deal rests on the communication skills of the merging parties, just as, in the long term, a healthy relationship between spouses or partners requires open and honest communication. Take Petruchio and Katherina. Not long married, but clearly with post-nuptial communication issues, Petruchio at first insists the sun is the moon, then—having persuaded Katherina of this—denounces her for agreeing with him that the moon is, in fact, the moon:

Nay, then you lie! It is the blessèd sun[7]

Not content with this, upon meeting an old man travelling along the same road, Petruchio says he sees a charming young maiden. Katherina agrees, adding for good measure that "she" is a "young budding virgin." Petruchio contradicts her again and she immediately concedes, pleading with the traveller:

Pardon, old father, my mistaking eyes.[8]

There is no stage direction for Katherina along the lines of "voice dripping with irony." But you could play it that way, suggesting at the very least a problematic relationship. After completing the then largest corporate merger in history

7 *The Taming of the Shrew*, Act 4, Scene 5, 17.
8 *The Taming of the Shrew*, Act 4, Scene 5, 45.

Steve Case and Gerald Levin, the leaders of America Online and Time Warner respectively, were soon pictured as a couple with a troubled affair on their hands. Their vision was of a global marriage of AOL's platform and Time Warner's content that would fundamentally change the media landscape. While "they really promised the moon" they delivered "very little of it."[9] AOL Time Warner's stock fell 70 per cent in less than three years. The platform people thought they could see the sun and the content people saw the whole of the moon, but the CEOs were left seeing stars.

Peter: *If we reveal our hand too soon there's a risk of exposing strategic vulnerabilities, particularly around governance issues in the post-merger scenario.*
Me: *Governance?*
Peter: *Yes, basic questions about who's in charge and the extent of their remit.*
Me: *Like who controls access to the tissues?*
Curtis: *Or who is seen to. In merger situations, perception is reality. The CEO has created a strong image of the synergies that could be realized through combining two entities.*
Me: *And the respective Boards have given assurances?*
Peter: *To a degree, since there remains some uncertainty about the nature of the merger.*
Me: *Meaning?*
Curtis: *Meaning, is it a vertical or a conglomerate …*
Peter: *… or a hostile bid?*

9 www.pbs.org/newshour/bb/business/july-dec02/aoltime_7-19.html.

Petruchio's approach to Katherina can be characterized as a "hostile take over,"[10] a concept that rings true when confronting the seemingly misogynistic assumptions in the play. Instead, it is possible to present Katherina as the one who wins out in the end, as Franco Zeffirelli does in his 1967 film starring that other sparky couple, Richard Burton and Elizabeth Taylor. Katherina makes her famous final speech, in which she pronounces her husband to be her lord, king and governor, and exhorts the other womenfolk to "unknit that threatening unkind brow." Petruchio cries "Come on and kiss me Kate!"—and kiss him she does, before slipping from his grasp and out the door.

The play's comedic and romantic intrigues can be framed as strategic questions similar to those in merger talks. Who's getting the best deal? Who's running the show? How much change has to be pushed through to make things work? In an acquisition one party to the deal ceases to exist, whereas in a merger both continue, albeit in altered form, and the impact upon each depends on the perception of which has gained the upper hand. Who has tamed who, you might say. In some cases it is far from clear whether one or the other is in charge or if the dominant role passes back and forth between them over time. A merger may seem more like an arranged marriage than a romantic one, but the cost of badly managed cultural integration in mergers has been reported at as much as 30 percent of overall performance. A cultural fit can be more important than a strategic fit in the long run.[11] So you could argue that the romantic takes precedence over the economic. Or, as Baptista puts it, that the merger should only go ahead

> *Ay, when the special thing is well obtained,*
> *That is, her love; for that is all in all.*[12]

Well, not quite all—there is the dowry, of course, and the assurances both of an income for the bride in the event of

---

10 Augustine & Adelman, op cit.

11 Dooley, K. & Zimmerman, B. (2003) Merger as marriage: communication issues in post-merger integration, *Journal of Health Care Management*, March, Lippincott, Williams & Wilkins.

12 *The Taming of the Shrew*, Act 2, Scene 1, 128–129.

her husband predeceasing her, and an inheritance for the groom from his father-in-law. Baptista promises Petruchio 20,000 crowns upfront for his merger with Katherina, and half of all his estate when he dies.

It dawns on me that Chris—my lunch date—has arrived and is smiling at me.

"You OK?"

"Yes, yes, I'm fine thanks. I was just discussing some merger and acquisition communication issues with Peter and Curtis here and …"

I trail off with a vague wave. There are many people around us, but not Peter and Curtis (should, by some incredible chance, those be their actual names). We start walking as we talk, and I guide Chris by the elbow toward the rather fine establishment where I have reserved a table overlooking the water. The maître d' ushers us in smoothly and we are soon seated and studying the menu. Chris leans back with the wine list, and I flip-flop silently between the cassoulet and the piperade.

In a relationship, it takes courage and determination to subject one's individuality to a combined existence with a partner. In the post-merger environment, the two combined cultures can clash, sometimes for years, until a new, composite culture emerges. The way couples talk to each other is cited as the single most accurate predictor for the longevity of a relationship, and there is a process of accommodation through which each learns to speak more like the other as a way of cementing the bond. But conformity, perhaps leading to subservience, can stifle the spark from which the match was struck. In business the same can happen when language is bent to particular goals. There are situations in which modern managers seek "to reinvent language with the objective of limiting thinking to a preconceived and often hidden agenda."[13] And, it has been suggested, the

13 Federman, M. & De Kerckhove, D. (2003) *McLuhan for Managers*, Viking Books, Toronto.

appropriation specifically of Shakespearean language by business—through management manuals, "inspirational" workshops and so on—while containing some progressive or even subversive possibilities, is a product of the imminent collapse in the cultural market value of Shakespeare on the one hand and, on the other, the vulnerability of capitalism in the wake of vast corporate scandals.[14]

"The white Bordeaux, I think," says Chris, knowing I'm paying. "You were saying something about language in mergers?"

"So I was, yes, of course. I'm with Karl Kraus on this," I say, struggling to remember what exactly I was saying, "when he said, 'Let men learn to serve language.'"

At which point we hear the butchered bars of Tarrega's Gran Vals—otherwise known as "the Nokia tune"—and I see Peter, who is seated at a table nearby with Curtis and a third man, pick up the call. Rather annoyingly, I find myself eavesdropping again.

> *"... take the example set by Reitzle and his team at Linde, following the successful merger of Linde and the BOC Group to create the Linde Group—a genuine global player ..."*[15]
>
> *"Genuine global player," I repeat mockingly, with a shrewish twist of my shoulders. "... perhaps not surprising," Peter continues loudly, "given that the advertising for the merger describes it as a match made in heaven."*

"Ha! There you have it," I declare, waving my fork triumphantly, "the merger as marriage."

Some time later, after a decent piperade has come and gone, our server appears again with a bottle of champagne.

---

14 Hendrick, D. (2004) The Bard of Enron: from shakespace to noir humanism, *College Literature*, October, West Chester University.

15 www.linde.com/merger.

"Compliments of the three gentlemen over there," she says, tipping her blonde chignon toward Peter and Curtis (and—could it be—Will?), "and there's a note." Astonished, I open it to reveal nothing but a mobile phone number. A prospective merger, I wonder, or a hostile bid?

And so to the Induction. *The Taming of the Shrew* features a rather strange piece of introductory business in which a drunkard is persuaded that he is in fact a lord, and memories of his previous life are but a bad dream. A company of travelling players arrives, seeking to entertain the household with a "pleasant comedy," meaning the *Shrew*. Leaving aside the temptation to ascribe to Shakespeare postmodern motives for such a self-referential device, casting the context for the main action in this way makes for a knowing audience. It creates a frame within a frame, and in doing so encourages us to think about the relationship between the events portrayed, the manner in which they are presented, and the audience for whom they are intended. This framing approach could serve well for business communicators as they support efforts to exploit the potential synergies between two sets of employees faced with becoming one. Placing the merger within a broader frame helps to create a common language and common ways of working. These commonalities are among the factors necessary to secure the staff buy-in and engagement upon which the long-term success of the merger depends.[16] Of all the original 26 in Shakespeare's company, John Hemmings may have best understood this. Actor, grocer and theatrical business manager, Hemmings would often have needed to foster engagement among the troupe in order to manage the changes imposed by venues and circumstances, and the demands of the works they performed. These works he then compiled, after Shakespeare's death, with fellow actor and creative partner Henry Condell. In their introductory epistle *To the great Variety of Readers* they observe of their departed friend that "His mind and hand went together: And what he

16 Internal communications during mergers and acquisitions: a checklist, www.eastbury.co.uk.

thought, he uttered with that easinesse, that wee have scarce received from him a blot in his papers."

Whether your papers are business or dramatic, corporate or poetic, to leave them with scarcely a blot seems to me a fine ambition.

The Tale of Two Statues

Elen Lewis on *The Winter's Tale*

Principal Actor: Augustine Phillips

Something happens in moments of silence. There's a crackle, a tension, a pulsating heartbeat as time moves on, while events stay still and calm. And something happens in moments of stillness. It's the pauses, the gaps, the stops, the hesitations, the breaks, the shhhhh ... that really say something. Something important. Silence becomes its own poetic language.

The Winter's Tale, my chosen Shakespeare play, is a study in silence. It's the story of Hermione, the queen banished and muffled for 16 years. Her return to the kingdom becomes a complex, theatrical trick when a statue becomes flesh. And in the final scene of the play, Shakespeare's soaring language transforms complexity and confusion into a moment of epiphany.

> Leontes: *There's magic in thy majesty, which has*
> *My evils conjured to remembrance, and*
> *From thy admiring daughter took the spirits*
> *Standing like stone with thee.*[1]

Stillness is also a poetic image. And the key is that doing nothing is itself an action, for movement can be evoked out of stillness. Consider postmodern architecture like the Guggenheim Bilbao, that shimmies and shimmers in the sunlight. Consider performers like living statues who stand

---

1 *The Winter's Tale*, Act 5, Scene 3, 39–42.

poised in a bubble of suspended animation, like Rodin creations. They're fluid, but still; silent but screaming.

What happens in dark, hidden, quiet corners is an intriguing space to explore. It can be a comforting, under-the-quilt place or somewhere that crackles with tension like a glaring spotlight on an empty stage. But it's a space, nonetheless, where things happen.

Scenes from an exhibition

I saw a living statue, face frozen with white clown paint, speed past on a bicycle. She whizzed down toward the London Embankment, crossing the river to join the exhibition of statues on the South Bank—mannequins, gladiators, green men, wizards and a golden angel with vast wings. All poised in ecosystems of suspense.

Stuart Louis is a living statue who dresses like a mannequin.[2] He says it makes him feel like a cyclone. There he is, still and silent in the centre, while there's movement all around. Spectators want to touch him, they want to feel his warmth. They want to feel flesh on flesh and answer the question: "Is this real?"

Being still and silent is not the same as being asleep. If you relax, you jerk, so there has to be a tension. Stuart keeps his eyes half open, that way he can have a sense of what's going on around him. He says it's an interesting place to be. "You're not participating," he explains, "but I can feel how the environment and atmosphere changes."

And he can't be too still. If he is, then people miss him. So, he has to come to life, just a little. And it's at this point in time that his audience change. He says they step forward and then they step backward, their eyes peeled wide open. It's as if they have to readjust to their own physicality, their own physical space. The moment of magic transfers onto the audience.

It is at these moments that Stuart loves being a living statue. He says it's a point of time when something, though he's not sure what, is being recognized. "There's a double-take and then people say, "Did you see that?" "It's a time

---

2 Stuart can be booked through www.continentaldrifts.co.uk.

alteration," he says, pausing. "Time can have a changing quality."

Matt Walters has been working as a frozen chimney sweep for 23 years, dressed in dungarees, a shirt and a flat hat.[3] Or sometimes, he's a white angel with six-foot wings. He can stand perfectly still for 30 minutes. He thinks he's good because of his marathon training. He's 42 years old and he can still run 40 miles. It means he's got a slow heartbeat, 32 beats a minute to be precise, which is handy when you're a living statue.

He may be standing still, but it's shattering. Sometimes his toes will spasm with the effort of it all. Or he'll get cramp in his calves or his tendon muscles. "If you throw energy out, you get energy back," he explains. "People will walk straight past when you're not putting out the energy."

But Matt loves people watching him. He loves the attention. "It's something to aspire to. I go into a little world and then I look up and hundreds of people are watching me," he says. "How do I stand so still? Anyone can. But you have to apply yourself."

He prefers older audiences though. He's had a few troubles with kids. He wonders if it's because they're spoilt with video games. They try and put him off and once or twice he's been attacked or spat at by youths in hoods.

There's a hidden barrier that exists between living statues and their audience. And it's not crossed until the performer finishes their work. The observers want to come and talk, they want to be part of it, they want to understand. Matt finds he gets lots of comments from his audience.

He wants to ask them, "Why are you watching a guy standing still?" He believes it's because there are realms of huge greatness in what he does. What he finds fascinating is crossing that barrier between his frozen self and the audience. It happens with his first movement, but he never plans it. It might be opening his eyes or he might touch someone. It all depends on the context. "What do I think about? Nothing at all. If I do, my heartbeat raises. It's like meditation."

The statue is a concept that continues to fascinate many artists. Desmond Jones is a founding father of physical

3 Matt can be booked through www.continentaldrifts.co.uk.

theatre and the founding director of the longest-running School of Mime and Physical Theatre in Britain.[4] "I teach people how to move, and a lot of them earn money by not moving, by being statues. I find the whole thing extraordinary. Very curious. What a strange thing to want to do. And what a very strange thing to want to watch," muses Jones.

Jones points out that the difference between good statues and bad statues lies in their quality of movement, even if that movement is stillness. While the boring statues are at rest, the interesting ones are working at not moving. "They have, like any good work of art, the breath of life," reveals Jones.

And then it is the quality of isolated movements that separates the wheat from the chaff. For movement is an orphan word. It needs something more to imbue it with quality, colour and character. "Do you move like water, clay or air?" questions Jones.

"I like your silence ..."

So what can business learn from the stories of the living statues and the inspiring moment of epiphany in the final scene of Shakespeare's *The Winter's Tale*? Well, quite simply, that silence is better than bad language. "I like your silence, it more shows off your wonder,"[5] says Paulina to her awed spectators as she reveals the statue of Hermione.

Even Shakespeare, a wordsmith, understands the power of silence, because silence itself requires many words. While *The Winter's Tale* characters are struck dumb by the vision of Hermione, a living statue, she too is quiet. There are competing silences on stage.

Paulina: *It appears she lives*
Though yet she speak not.[6]

It is unusual for Shakespeare to disguise crucial information from his audience. Yet in this instance, it is the spectators

---

4 Desmond Jones is writing a book on mime, which will include a chapter on statues, www.desmondjones.com.

5 *The Winter's Tale*, Act 5, Scene 3, 21–22.

6 *The Winter's Tale*, Act 5, Scene 3, 117.

as well as the characters that have been led to believe Hermione is dead. A moment of magic is needed. A poetic image, some poetic language is required to create an epiphany. And Shakespeare achieves this through silence, stillness and suspended animation, until Hermione's statue slowly thaws and comes to life.

> Paulina: *Music; awake her—strike!*
> *'Tis time; descend; be stone no more;*
> *Approach;*
> *Strike all that look upon with marvel.*[7]

And those businesses that are succinct, sometimes silent, that use gaps and pauses to punctuate meaning are wise communicators. It's an ability that recreates the magic that occurs between living statues and their audience, and it's the same suspense that occurs in the final scene of *The Winter's Tale*.

The pause is one of the researcher's most powerful tactics in focus groups. It's also a vital negotiation tool in business and in real life. I once had a boss whose pregnant pauses were notorious and irritating, yet incredibly effective. During his studied periods of silence I would chatter away, digging a deeper hole for myself.

As an interviewing technique, silence works. Many a chief executive and marketing director have unveiled surprising revelations during silence. The journalist who rushes in to fill a pause will miss out on these moments of insight.

In China, long silences are an important part of communication. *The Economist* counsels international advisers to remain unnerved. A great wall of silence can be unsettling but it's a deft tool when used by a skilled negotiator.

Long silences when the air sets still can be powerful. But learn from the living statues. Their poise and energy creates a suspended animation. It's like actors on a stage. If they forget their lines and hold a strong posture then the audience will still believe in them.

So stillness and silence can create suspense, an ingredient that modern business could do with a pinch of. Suspense

7 *The Winter's Tale*, Act 5, Scene 3, 98–100.

enables the observer to go on their own voyage, it enables an audience's imagination to take over. In the creative process, a willing suspension of disbelief is essential. It's the thing that reverberates. It's when ripples of meaning flow beyond the original sense of the word.

Ron East is the director of the London School of Mime and he believes that suspended energy is crucial. "For the mime artist it's a place of simplicity. For the actor they're always looking for that moment when everything becomes effortless. Everyone's looking for that moment," he says.

"You speak a language that I understand not"

The Winter's Tale also teaches us of the danger of miscommunication. At the beginning of the drama, Hermione is sentenced to death by her husband, King Leontes, a tragic hero consumed with raving jealousy. He is wrongly convinced of her infidelity and nothing will change his mind. Shakespeare demonstrates the chasm in miscommunication between husband and wife by juxtaposing the measured, clear language of Hermione, with the crazed monologues of Leontes.

Hermione: *You speak a language that I understand not.*
My life stands in the level of your dreams,
Which I'll lay down.
Leontes: *Your actions are my dreams.*[8]

There are countless occasions in business when miscommunication or a strange language has led to a complete lack of understanding, perhaps internally or between a brand and its consumers. There are the amusing tales of globalization gone wrong, such as IKEA's worldwide product naming program that caused offence in Germany with a bed called "Gutvik," which translates as "good fuck."

Similarly, many brands come unstuck during the complex renaming process in China. Detached from the security of the Roman alphabet, there are many pitfalls. Pizza Hut's Chinese name translated as "must win customers," while Microsoft's was "tiny/soft, weak."[9]

---

8 *The Winter's Tale*, Act 3, Scene 2, 77–80.
9 Dr Ying Fan in *Brand Strategy* magazine, 22/04/02.

But more seriously, the sort of garbled language that Leontes speaks during his raving jealousy is remarkably similar to some of the incoherent communication used by business. Shakespeare uses bad language to neatly illustrate madness, jealousy and a confused mind. Consider Leontes' raving monologue where he cries:

> *Why then the world and all that's in't is nothing*
> *The covering sky is nothing, Bohemia nothing,*
> *My wife is nothing, nor nothing have these nothings*
> *If this be nothing.*[10]

And businesses that use muddled language may be veiling confusion and complexity. There is similar repetition, long sentences and incomprehension in Wanadoo UK's terms and conditions, a Golden Bull winner in last year's plain English awards. (Golden Bulls are examples of bad language, rather than good.)

> *The failure to exercise or delay in exercising a right or remedy under this Agreement shall not constitute a waiver of the right or remedy or a waiver of any other rights or remedies and no single or partial exercise of any right or remedy under this Agreement shall prevent any further exercise of the right or remedy or the exercise of any other right or remedy.*[11]

The stark link between clear language and clear strategy is illuminated during an analysis of the readability of letters to shareholders from major US companies. While the most readable came from Lou Gerstner at IBM, Jack Welch at General Electric, and Larry Page and Sergey Brin at Google, the least readable included Ken Lay and Jeffrey Skilley at Enron, Garry Winnick at Global Crossing and Richard Grasso at NYSE—all companies involved in scandal and corruption.[12]

---

10 *The Winter's Tale*, Act 1, Scene 2, 190–192.

11 www.plainenglish.co.uk/goldenbulls.

12 Fugere, B., Hardaway, C. & Warshawsky, J. (2005) *Why Business People Speak Like Idiots: A Bullfighter's Guide*, p. 45.

Candyfloss words

When people write in a way that is hard to read or unclear, they have something to hide. And the problem with wasted words is that they're like candyfloss—there's nothing there when you bite into them. Shakespeare understood that words aren't always necessary.

Modern business seems to feel obliged to fill space. Instead, it should stay quiet and still and let silence speak for it. Sometimes, candyfloss words attempt to hide deception. So, the businessman who doesn't want to lie but can't tell the truth either, must chatter away about nothing at all. Yet the banality of the language reveals more than it should—namely that the organization has nothing to say, or something to hide.

Brands that I admire use simple, prosaic language, like Hermione's when she tried to defend herself on trial. They don't fall into the trap of speaking a corporate language that none of their consumers will understand. The following message was written on a carton of soup at Pret A Manger and succinctly describes the fast food chain's values.

> *A while ago, a consumer phoned me to say our soup was good but not amazing. The gauntlet was down.*
>
> *I tracked down and engaged (full time) the UK's premier soup guru and cook book writer, Nick Sandler. Together we changed our recipes, our broth, our ingredients and cooking methods. We took on and trained new soup chefs.*
>
> *Thank you to that lady who called. (Sorry but I've lost your number.)*
>
> *If you're reading this, I hope you agree we rose to the challenge. Do let me know what you think, and thanks again.*
>
> *Signed, Julian Metcalfe*[13]

There are times when language is really important, and times when it is not so. There are times when modern business degrades language and it dulls us, deadens us. But there will always be writers, like Shakespeare, who surpass them-

13 www.wheresthesausage.typepad.com.

selves and recover the meaning of language again. They create suspense.

It's time for business to find the common language that reverberates meaning. And the first simple step is to understand the importance of standing still and saying nothing at all.

Will Kemp's Nine Days' Wonder

Jamie Jauncey on *Romeo and Juliet*

Principal Actor: William Kemp

PROLOGUE—March 1599

London

Damn that egghead Shakerags. Damn him and his mincing troupe of tragedy-mongers. A pox on their lofty ideals, their playing to the gallery. Damn their Globule too, verminous rackety pit that it is. They can keep it. I want no share of it any longer.

A clown! Their lips curl at the thought. *A dancer!* Old Shaky inspects the tip of his quill—but only for an instant—before striking fat Falstaff from his history of *Henry the Fifth*. Knowing full well it would have been my hour of triumph. My star outshining every one of theirs.

Jealous they are, Shagpoke, Buggerage and the rest. Jealous that folk push into the theatre at the end of the plays just to see my jig. That's the truth of it. So damn them all and good riddance, I say. I quit. Today I, Will Kemp, leave the Chamberlain's Men for ever.

But they're the losers. It's Will Kemp who can speak to the common folk. With his bawdy jests and merry dances and mad capers. Nor shall I let it go to waste. Oh no. I'll take ... let me see ... *Romeo and Juliet*, aye ... and make some mischief of my own with that piffling tale. For it's plain as piecrust there was rottenness abroad even then. The piss-poor part that penny-poet wrote me. Peter, the Nurse's man. Pah. Two short scenes. Blink and you'd miss me. And that ending:

For never was a story of more woe
Than this of Juliet and her Romeo

Ripe cheese. Though it filled even the groundlings' gobs for once. Had them snivelling into their sleeves. How was I to do my jig after that, pray? Simply stroll on stage and warm them up again like cold pease porridge …?

But I'm a charitable man. I'll not dwell on the past. A nine days' wonder! That's what I'll give them. Show them Will Kemp may be a Chamberlain's Man no more, but he still has something to excite. God's blood, he has! With *Romeo and Juliet* in his pocket for a jape. I'll leave them jaws agape as I dance myself out of the world …

DAY ONE—June 2006

Birnam Wood

A fog before mine eyes. What place is this? How came I to be here? All is confused. My garb is strange, and stranger still my thoughts. No marching trees are these. No King Macbeth waits yonder now upon Dunsinane Hill. Though lo, the final remnant of his doom still stands, a lone millennial oak. And yet, I thought the star-crossed lovers were my wish. But hold. The fog doth lift. My mind grows clear. I live here now. This is the world to which my merry dance hath brought me. And, 'tis plain, archaic thoughts and speech have no place in't. Fivefold iambs snare the modern tongue …

DAY TWO—June 2006

Birnam Village, Kemp's place

Unh … that felt strange … dreamlike, almost … ah well … stress, maybe. Codswallop, Kemp. Ecstasy, more likely. For yesterday, the battle of Wills came to an end. And I, Will Kemp, quit Chamberlain's. They cited "artistic differences." I cite disappearing up their own arses.

"You've what?" asks my financial adviser. "You've handed over your equity in the building? That, Will, was not your smartest move."

"Look, Beans," I reply, "I've knocked around this business for an age. I've seen it before. There comes a moment when it's time to get back to what you do best and … frankly … to hell with the money."

"So what *are* you going to do?" he asks.

I smile.

"Something wonderfully weird. Just wait and see."

DAY THREE—June 2006

South Gyle, Edinburgh

Reception at Scottish & Newcastle plc's headquarters is a far cry from Chamberlain's rathole premises. It is, in fact, Starbucks by any other name. People chat at the coffee bar, lounge in leather seats, sip their lattes, talk brands.

"How would you like," I ask my quarry, "to help me with a project? Something … um … a little out of the ordinary …"

She raises a suspicious eyebrow.

"Shakespeare," I continue. "*Romeo and Juliet*. What it tells you about your job. About Scottish & Newcastle. About the drinks industry."

"I *hate* Shakespeare," she says.

"So do I." I spare her the details. "But it could be interesting. For your team. Internal Communications. If ever there were a tale about the consequences of bad communication, this is it."

I see the possibilities turning in her mind.

"Do what with it, exactly?" Suspicion lingers.

"Read it. Go and see it. Think about it. Maybe even write something about it."

"Hmmm."

"Montague and Capulet. Opposite sides of a feud. Scottish & Newcastle. Opposite sides of the Tweed," I venture lamely.

She grimaces.

"We'll call it Project Shaky," she says. Leaving me to draw my own conclusions.

DAY FOUR—July 2006

Birnam Village, Kemp's place again

There. I've read it again. Though I nearly choked on it. And I skipped Peter's parts.

So ... who do we have? The star-crossed lovers themselves: spoilt, randy, narcissistic and underage. Tybalt: a thug. Mercutio: ditto, but cleverer. Benvolio: a goody-goody. Paris: a halibut. Capulet and Montague: a pair of ridiculous old fighting cocks. Their wives: one frigid, the other hysterical. The Prince: a stuffed shirt. The Nurse: a fishwife, but with less sense. The Friar: an idiot and a coward to boot. In sum, a cast of retards and a plot to make your eyes water. What in God's name are my new friends at Scottish & Newcastle going to make of all this?

Only time will tell. Meanwhile, to work. For my quarry-turned-fellow conspirator, mother hen to her little brood of communicators, the Nurse is tempting, but too obvious. The Friar, then, edgier, more unreliable. Next ...

DAY FIVE—September 2006

South Gyle, a meeting room

There are six maids and two knaves in the internal communications team. I start by allocating the parts, making no concessions to age, beauty or gender. If anyone is disappointed they hide it well.

Now to the mischief proper. They are first to read Shakerags' misbegotten drama. Next, we'll sally forth to Stratford and endure a performance. Last, if still in possession of their wits, they are to write a piece that explores how they relate, or fail to relate, to their character, and what that character might say to them about business life. It can be an essay, a story, a poem, a diary entry, a dialogue, a suite of haikus, a limerick scrawled on a beermat, or anything else they feel inspired to write; but it should be a personal and creative response to the experience of getting to know the character and the play.

There is audible relief when I say I will be on hand for support and advice if anyone gets stuck.

I leave them looking enthused but somewhat thunderstruck.

DAY SIX—September 2006

Stratford-upon-Avon

A hitch. Romeo, Mercutio, the Nurse, the Friar, the Prince/Paris and I are stranded at Edinburgh Airport. Rain lashes down. Out on the tarmac nothing moves. I should have known something was up when the departures screen read Gate 14. The previous week there was no Gate 14.

The clock ticks by: 10.00. 10.30. 11.00. 11.30. The curtain rises at 14.00. The Capulets are flying from Glasgow. Juliet is driving from Hereford. Tybalt/Benvolio is on the way from Didcot.

We sit at Gate 14, watching the rain, and talk. They have all read the play now. Almost all have found it hard going. As tiered and laden with meaning as business-speak, their daily currency, is one-dimensional and colourless.

Midday. On board now but we are waiting, says the steward, for a consignment of wet fish bound for Spain. From Scotland. By air. Via Birmingham. Somewhere in there is a Shakespearean irony. But before we can dredge it up the captain announces that we will fly without the fish.

We land 40 minutes later and call Capulet on his mobile. The performance has been delayed by 20 minutes. We make haste for Stratford.

Act 1, Scene 2 is ending as we arrive. It's fortunate that they've read the play. We find our seats, the warm theatre darkness closes in around us and brand wars, the off-trade, airports and wet fish are quickly forgotten, driven from our minds by the movement and lighting, the stave-dance fights and slapstick, the music, the rage and passion.

This, they agree afterwards, is how Shaky's language *should* be put to work. By actors who lift it from the page and breathe life into it. They have all, they readily admit, been transported. The conversation is animated as we make our way back to the airport. Even I am forced to admit that whatever his shortcomings, when Shakerags makes with the words, he's good. Very good indeed.

DAY SEVEN—October 2006

South Gyle, a banter deck

Three weeks have passed. We meet in what is quaintly called "the banter deck," a café-style room with large windows, on whose walls hang coyly drink-free images of people bantering merrily. I review work-in-progress with four of the cast.

Mercutio has almost completed a short story about the betrayal felt by a long-serving drayman who is transferred along with part of the business when it is sold. She has written it in the Edinburgh vernacular. It's funny and touching and captures Mercutio's linguistic exuberance and quickness to anger. Romeo's role as the drayman's manager still needs clarifying.

Juliet has cast herself as a spoilt air-head whose godfather, the manager, has wangled her a job in the ordering department. Confused when asked to cover for an admiring colleague, she turns to the friendly but bungling Mr Friar who advises her to feign absence, which she does with disastrous consequences. We agree that her character needs to reflect a little more at the end.

Romeo has imagined herself as a new low-alcohol, citrus-flavoured spritzer "of complex character" from Montague Drinks Ltd. Targeted at 18- to 30-year-old women, Romeo will be pitched against Tybalt, a similar product from Capulets Inc. The promotional campaigns include a Masquerade Ball and a Find-the-love-of-your-life reality TV show. The piece only lacks a conclusion.

The Friar has a natural ear for the comic, but she's given herself a hard task, retelling his story in the verse style of another William: the Scottish anti-bard, McGonagall. We decide that this sets too many constraints, even if consistency of rhyme and metre are not amongst them. She needs to find an alternative approach.

I leave impressed with the work that has gone into these pieces. My players all have demanding jobs to do, as well. But on the evidence so far, I think my mischief is working.

DAY EIGHT—October 2006

The same banter deck

Two weeks later and we're back at South Gyle in congratulatory mood. Romeo, Juliet and Mercutio have ended their pieces with flourishes worthy of Shakerags himself.

The Friar has settled for a monologue in which she likens her grappling for understanding of old Shaky to a gruelling session at the gym. Her character, she concludes, is a dangerous halfwit; and, she adds, having herself worked in three FTSE-100 companies, she has witnessed at first hand precisely the kind of shenanigans that go on in the play.

The Nurse knows nannies, having had several herself. But this one deceives her when, as a precocious young reader, she is seduced by the apparent affection Shaky's character lavishes on her charge. Later, the scales fall from her eyes as she realizes how badly the Nurse has let Juliet down. Finally, though, she is reconciled. Her character is simply a bawd, a gossip and the epitome of bad communication—and so to be found wherever two or more are gathered together ...

The Prince reflects on his character's shortcomings as arbitrator and meter-out-of-justice. The avoidance of internecine strife, he concludes, calls for an eagle eye, a sympathetic ear, an open mind, and a fair serving of charm. Paris, meanwhile, will never get the girl till he stops making assumptions and starts asking questions and listening.

At Captastic Inc, the Capulets have a problem. The chief executive wants to revamp the ailing product line and go global, the chairman wishes to preserve the status quo. They are so busy arguing they fail to foresee the collapse of their market, their enforced merger with their competitors, and the subsequent acquisition of Capmont by Snapthemup Inc.

Tybalt/Benvolio, meanwhile, has sent her characters on an Influencing Skills workshop. A furious Tybalt is assiduously failing to learn by Benvolio's example that listening and empathizing gets better results than belabouring people about the ears with a cudgel.

For some reason this seems a fitting note on which to end. As we leave for a celebratory pizza (what else?) I have the impression that my cast of players have enjoyed themselves. They might even, I flatter myself, care for more of Will Kemp's mischief in the future.

DAY NINE—November 2006

Kemp's place

So ends my Nine Days' Wonder. Time will tell whether I have achieved what I set out to do, namely season the corporate broth, sow some seeds of enquiry, expansion, perhaps even enlightenment—with Shakerags' execrable tale as compost.

I am pleased that my players found enjoyment in it. More pleased still that most found it stretching. Thrown together in the experience of something well outside the business norm, their imaginations were exercised in a manner that has little licence in their daily work. Hard though the language proved, it struck a fine contrast with the banality, the utter meaninglessness even, of management-speak. And if there are indeed Montagues and Capulets, Mercutios and Tybalts, Romeos and Juliets, Nurses and Friars in most organizations, their familiar character types were brought into sharper focus through the unfamiliar lens of the play.

And where am I, Will Kemp, now? The richer for my players' acquaintance, that is certain. Grateful, though it sticks in my craw to say it, to old Shakerags for his genius with language. *My only love sprung from my only hate*, to borrow Juliet's line. But was I right to quit? Oh yes. The tide had turned against me. I am an old dog now, and Chamberlain's men were trying new tricks. But even old dogs have their day. And these nine days of wonder have been mine. Mark my words, though, they will not be my last …

EPILOGUE—November 2006

Birnam Village

Will Kemp was the great clown of his day and a fine comic actor. Following the main performances he frequently took to the stage with a jig, a short improvised play featuring bawdy jokes, knockabout acting and dancing. A founder member of the Chamberlain's Men, he paid £100 for a share in the Globe. But as Shakespeare's sophistication grew, Kemp's style began to seem rustic and antiquated. In 1599 he quit and his stake was taken up by the other shareholders. A year later he returned to his roots in nine days of morris dancing that took him, over a period of a month, from London to Norwich, attended by large crowds. He later published a pamphlet, *Kemps nine daies vvonder*, in which he wrote, "I have daunst my selfe out of the world"—which might have been a punning reference to his exit from the Globe. For all his earlier fame, he died penniless in 1603. "Kempe, a man" said the Southwark burial record simply.

Inevitable Incompetence

Nicola David on *Measure for Measure*

Principal Actor: Thomas Pope

Strip cartoons lose a little something in the describing, but bear with me. If you're a Dilbert fan, you'll enjoy this anyway (and if not, why not?).

OK, picture the scene: Dogbert says to a pointy-haired induhvidual,[1] "Today I will teach you how to use your incompetence to achieve your goals." As the cartoon progresses, we discover that Step 1 is easy enough: just be incompetent. Steps 2 through 6 involve things like volunteering for the most difficult and important projects; insisting that competent people be pulled off other projects to help us; and claiming credit for their work. And in Step 7, after we get promoted, we fire them—to eliminate witnesses.

Was Scott Adams inspired by *Measure for Measure*? I'm afraid to ask, in case he ridicules my presumption and draws an embarrassing cartoon about me. (Who am I kidding? I'd love that: I'd dine out on it until I exploded.) I'll just take a guess and say he wasn't. More likely, I imagine—and herein lies the reason for his success—Adams simply shares Shakespeare's ability to observe and dissect human nature, and exploit it for the purpose of entertainment. Cartoonist, bard ... same thing, really.

---

1 "Induhvidual" is the Dilbert word for a person who's very stupid. Ones with pointy hair are the worst. Dilbert cartoons are © Scott Adams, Inc and distributed by United Feature Syndicate, Inc. See this cartoon at www.dilbert.com: click on 5 November 2006 in the archive.

Context and environment may affect our words and actions (you might eat peas from your knife at home, but refrain during dinner with the Archbishop of Canterbury, for example), but they can't really affect our characters—the essence of who and what we really are. So although Adams expresses himself through a twenty-first-century business context, the people in his cubicles have all the same foibles as characters in Shakespeare's plays.

The Dilbert cartoon I reference picks up on a hypothesis put forward in the satirical 1969 book *The Peter Principle*[2] (subtitled, like the user guide to the Hubble Telescope, "Why Things Always Go Wrong"). The authors suggest that, in a hierarchy, every employee tends to rise to his or her level of incompetence.

There's a dilemma around the practical interpretation of the Peter Principle: should the rule be allowed to come into play naturally, or be forced? (Indeed, the contemporary twist on the rule seems to be: when going for a new job or an internal promotion, you should *aim* to be promoted to your level of incompetence.)

In other words, should we only go for jobs that we can already do hands down, or should we aim higher, in order to obtain—and *then* justify—greater pay, prestige, power and prospects? After all, if a new job's as easy as the one we're already doing, is it really a promotion? And maybe we're just too lazy to develop in advance the skills we're going to need later.

All of this is why people work hard at "spinning" their accomplishments, and embellishing (I'm being kind, here) their CVs. Because in the dog-eat-dog corporate world, you've got to appear capable of doing a job you're not capable of doing so that you can get the job you want in order to learn to be capable of doing it. Clear?

It was to Shakespeare. He was ahead of the game on the Peter Principle, as demonstrated by the main characters in *Measure for Measure*. Like many of his plays, this one is about power. Unlike many of the others, it's much less about the abuse of power or position than the inability to

2 *The Peter Principle: Why Things Always Go Wrong* by Laurence J. Peter & Raymond Hull, William Morrow & Company, Inc, New York, 1969.

cope with them (for which, read "incompetence"). And people really haven't changed in the 400 years since the play was first staged.

In a 2006 survey for NatWest,[3] 43 per cent of respondents said they could do a better job than their boss. Incompetence on the part of the boss, or wishful thinking from the respondents? Either way, it underlines what Shakespeare and Adams knew and used to their advantage—that everyone has weaknesses that affect their performance, and that those weaknesses are there to be exploited. And they matter—the implication of the Peter Principle is that "the organization is prone to collapse when the number of incompetents among its ranks reaches a critical mass, resulting in the inability of the organization to perform its functions."[4]

As individuals, perhaps we should exercise caution as to how high we aim: it's all too easy to ignore our own weaknesses, and to avoid judging our own behaviour. And so we can easily come unstuck. Perfectly ordinary people are wont to send their lives off the rails—often quite spectacularly—when finding themselves in sudden possession of power of any kind, such as knowledge, trust, position, talent, wealth, beauty or celebrity.

A well-intentioned congressman rises to become an intern-seducing President, just as an earnest young MP one day becomes the Home Secretary who pays for his lover's train fare with a parliamentary warrant. The nobody jilted lover of a public figure sells her story to the tabloids; an already-champion cyclist boosts his performance pharmaceutically; a man who once heard a calling from God becomes a child-abusing priest. An unremarkable young woman wrecks her own life upon winning the lottery; a starry-eyed ingénue grows into the A-lister whose septum collapses under the weight of all that cocaine. Did these people set out to do these things? Probably not. They probably just lost perspective.

In a business context, serious incompetence is no fun for anyone: not for any stakeholder, and certainly not for

3 "You're the Business", a survey of *Red* magazine readers for NatWest Bank, 2006.

4 *Peter Principle*, Wikipedia, at en.wikipedia.org/wiki/Peter_Principle.

colleagues above, below and around the individual, or for themselves. Duck-like, they must paddle very hard beneath the surface. They must expend considerable energy on projecting the correct image while simultaneously avoiding detection, and they need a variety of damage-limitation strategies if they're to avoid public humiliation.

As recruiting employers, can we identify and exclude the worst candidates for incompetence by depending on interviews, or our knowledge of already having worked with them? Both of these rely heavily on measures of *past* performance, and may be poor indicators of future behaviour once people have crossed their own incompetence threshold (as predicted by *The Peter Principle*).

So might we use psychological tests to gauge a candidate's likely ability to cope with power or position? HR specialists waver as to the usefulness of psychometric testing, although a new three-dimensional grid, developed by Germany's Chemnitz University of Technology and presented at a conference in November 2006, promises to "translate a person's gut instincts into a rich picture of personality."[5] However, "The truth is that no organizational assessment or survey is perfect; even those of the highest psychometric quality can only produce feedback that is based on mathematical extrapolations (as reliable as these may be)," write Houran, Lange and Ference.[6] I rather suspect Shakespeare would mock the idea of science as a measure for character.

Perhaps when combined with personal coaching and mentoring, testing *can* help to select the most appropriate candidate for a role—and then keep them on track. Yet this, in turn, has implications for the competence of the testers, coaches and mentors!

The ideal (but unattainable) test, and one of which Enron stakeholders must regularly dream, is to have Shakespeare cast each candidate in a play, light the blue touchpaper, and retire to the safety of the gallery—from where we can observe without fear of corporate or personal

---

5 Psychometrics without prejudice, *The Economist*, 9 November 2006.

6 *Beware of Barnum and Forer Effects in Organizational Assessments* by James Houran, Rense Lange and Gene A. Ference, 21 September 2006.

damage. Certainly, we are fascinated by wrongdoing in others, imagining that we can do no wrong while vicariously living in a world more dangerous and consequential than our own. "Evil is alluring, and not just to those who would dramatize it. From mild naughtiness to vicious criminality, the performance of bad deeds is something the rest of the population evidently wants to know about," wrote Bruce Weber in the *New York Times.*[7] Shakespeare was only too happy to oblige.

Like Scott Adams and, in fact, many a boss, Shakespeare treats his *Measure for Measure* characters with a kind of benevolent malice. The most powerful man in Vienna, the Duke, is clearly incompetent, failing right, left and centre. He even shies away from the limelight: "I love the people, but do not like to stage me to their eyes."

The Duke uses the most tortuous language and syntax to cover up his lack of self-confidence. You probably recognize the type: only the least secure managers feel the need to use complex business jargon to try to conjure up an intellectual chasm between themselves and their reader/listener. The more insecure they are, the more incomprehensible the verbiage. Adams knows the type: "We must develop knowledge optimization initiatives to leverage our key learnings," says the induhvidual. "Smart," thinks the clueless listener.

As a third measure of his incompetence, the Duke tries to win friends and influence people by avoiding getting tough with them: "We have strict statutes and most biting laws ... which for this fourteen years we have let slip." Caught between the pleasure of prestige and the pressure of power, the Duke isn't fit for the job. (Sound like any managers you know?)

Yet Shakespeare allows the Duke to come good in the end.

Angelo's incompetence has more serious implications. Deputized to stand in for the Duke in his absence, Angelo lets his new-found power go to his head—condemning a man to death for a minor misdeed and extorting sex from the prisoner's sister (a convent novice!) in exchange for his freedom. Just as rape is about control rather than lust, sexual

---

7 *Cozying up to the psychopath that lurks deep within*, Bruce Weber in the *New York Times*, 10 February 1991.

harassment (in the workplace, as elsewhere) is about power. It's an all-too-familiar theme: in the 2005/2006 financial year, sexual harassment ranked as one of the top five reasons for calls to the British Equal Opportunities Commission helpline,[8] and the Industrial Relations Service found that, in one year, harassment complaints had been made in 54 per cent of organizations.[9]

As for young nun Isabella, it's a horrific shock to discover the sexual power she wields: Angelo is seduced by her piety, and the Duke goes on to unexpectedly propose in the final scene. Overwhelmed and ill-equipped, Isabella chooses to place a higher value on her chastity than on her brother's life.

These main characters, then, are unable to cope with their positions or power—and find themselves operating beyond their own competence. This is what the play is all about, as the Duke suggests: "Hence shall we see, if power changes purpose, what our seemers be."

Anyone who's ever been in business will know that power is a fickle and slippery thing, often residing where you least expect. It is given and stolen in strategic alliances, in the appointment of stooges, in the negotiation of blame, and in the cunning manipulation of people, position and process—all in the pursuit of agendas both personal and corporate.

Which, in turn, means that power frequently ends up in the hands of those least equipped to cope. And along with it can come a compounding sense of invincibility. As Angelo said when Isabella threatened to tell all: "Who will believe thee, Isabel? My unsoiled name, th'austereness of my life, my vouch against you, and my place i'th'state, will so your accusion overweigh ..."

Throughout *Measure for Measure*, Shakespeare retains compassion for such characters, seeing them as incompetent "goodies" gone astray rather than inherent "baddies" intent

---

8 *Sally Bing Awarded £58,697 in Sexual Harassment Case Against Former Town Mayor*, Equal Opportunities Commission press release dated 6 October 2006.

9 *Sexual Harassment at Work 1: Incidence and Outcomes*, Industrial Relations Service (1996a), IRS Employment Trends 615 pp. 4–10.

on doing ill. Consider his choice of name for Angelo: Lucifer was a favourite among heaven's angels, but plummeted from glory when he tried to lead a coup against God. As a longtime member of the heavenly host, he already held considerable power; his undoing was in letting it go to his head. Certainly, Angelo's soliloquies reflect his inner conflict, rather than a bent on doing evil. We're back to the idea of benevolent malice: Angelo's actions are despicable, but Shakespeare opens wide the door on his humanity and vulnerability.

It's important to understand that *Measure for Measure* is classified as one of Shakespeare's "problem plays." Samuel Johnson and Coleridge both slated it,[10] and the *Advanced York Notes* offer this: "Of all Shakespeare's plays, it is the one which is most insistently full of questions … and correspondingly light on answers.… Until the second half of the twentieth century, *Measure for Measure* was not a popular play."[11]

The reason it was unpopular, and why this point is important, is that Shakespeare remains uncharacteristically silent about his stage of flawed characters. The people we take to be villains are treated compassionately by both playwright and fellow protagonists, and ultimately redeemed. Several of the people we take to be "goodies" make dreadful decisions or are simply ridiculous. There is no stark black or white. The Victorians wanted a strong moral stance: they didn't get it. Even today, scholars can't agree whether this is a tragedy (starts well, ends badly) or a comedy (starts badly, ends well). Yet as difficult as the play may be, it hasn't fallen by the wayside. In a perverse way, we continue to relish its challenges.

Measure for Measure demands a response: pick a moral stance, any moral stance, as long as you're prepared to defend it—and to cast the first stone. It's up to us, as individuals (or induhviduals). This is why the play remains particularly timeless. The foibles and failings of Shakespeare's characters endure, as do the questions he poses; giving no

---

10 *The Plays of William Shakespeare*, Samuel Johnson, 1765; *Coleridge's Shakespearean Criticism*, T. M. Raysor, 1930.

11 *York Notes Advanced on "Measure for Measure" by William Shakespeare*, 2003 edn, Emma Smith.

answers, he avoids date-stamping himself on any moral timeline.

His main point, I believe, is that no one in the audience can claim to be any better than his characters. And if *he* won't judge them, by punishing them as he perhaps ought, is he suggesting we also refrain from judging those around us? No—I suspect Shakespeare's tolerance and compassion are clear indicators that it is only in being one another's keepers that we can find protection from the actions of ourselves and others, and the support and forgiveness we need to get through it all.

Shakespeare and Adams have the luxury of being able to poke their characters until they react, and parading the results, without coming under scrutiny themselves. In the workplace, none of us has that advantage. Here, our weaknesses are exposed and the potential consequences can be dramatic—particularly if we have the ill fortune to be set against a highly political backdrop. We cannot indulge in judging others unless we are equally prepared to judge ourselves, and to be judged. It is in being compassionate and forgiving that we can access compassion and forgiveness for ourselves.

Measure for Measure shows that each of us has an incompetence threshold, but Shakespeare's hand is light, and he offers redemption. As business people, we can learn from this. In turn, through Dilbert, Adams inspires us to find humour and friendship in the midst of weakness, however surreal: both are important workplace survival tools.

We should take care to apportion responsibility wisely, and accept it cautiously. There is no room for complacency at either end of the power spectrum. As Shakespeare dramatizes through his plays, the human condition—for both leaders and the led—is essentially one of weakness, even in apparent strength. Angelo himself conceded: "We are all frail." For both personal and corporate success, it's important to continually measure ourselves and one another, dosing those measures with compassion, humour and forgiveness, and looking more to humanity than science. And we must accept judgement as we judge—measure for measure.

Who Moved My Mousetrap?

John Bolton on *Hamlet*

Principal Actor: George Bryan

To buy in, or not to buy in? That is the question in a business world where jargon exerts an increasing stranglehold. Imagine *Hamlet* rewritten in business buzzwords: Polonius would be a "champion of best practice." The Gravedigger would be encouraged to "think outside the box." Fortinbras would consider Denmark a "good strategic fit." And Hamlet would be accused of "failing to embrace change."

You don't have to subject Shakespeare to such treatment to recognize that much of this jargon is "weary, stale, flat and unprofitable," as Hamlet might say. Yet many businesses use it with unthinking enthusiasm. In a typical office—an environment no less introspective than the court of Denmark in Shakespeare's play—people take their lead from the top and jargon spreads rapidly. Before you know it, you're sitting in a meeting trying to find ways to "push the envelope." Those of us who use jargon sardonically aren't doing ourselves any favours. Jargon is still jargon, whether or not it is surrounded by ironic inverted commas.

This warping of the English language is bad enough in the business world, but jargon is seeping into everyday life. Microwave dinners have become "meal solutions" and children's nurseries have "vision statements." There are probably people who go on dates with the aim of "leveraging synergies"—or maybe that's just in Canary Wharf.

The popularity of business jargon should come as no surprise. Everyone wants to succeed at work and by using the latest buzzwords we confirm that we're committed members of the corporate club. A common language—however hackneyed—suggests common ideals. In a sense, jargon has become part of the script for the role we perform at the office. By scattering a few words of jargon into our conversations and emails, we think we'll end each day to the sound of rapturous applause.

Businesses think this language makes them sound smart and efficient—but does it really? Mainly, jargon is used to dress up the bland and just plain obvious, at the very most adding a thin veneer of urgency. It's no surprise that businesses want to do things quickly, but do they really need to translate that simple goal into a phrase of jargon like "execute at pace"? Are organizations embarrassed by the apparent simplicity of their vision? Perhaps they think their employees are more likely to respond to words that are unfamiliar and corporate-sounding?

Whatever the reasons, such phrases quickly gain currency in an organization. Whether or not you're "executing at pace" becomes a secondary issue, it seems. What matters is how often you use the phrase.

Perhaps it's unfair to contrast such mechanical and dull jargon with the sublime, imaginative language we find in Shakespeare's work. After all, it is not the job of businesses to craft lines that will be quoted four hundred years hence. But the contrast underlines what is missing from jargon—namely, anything that sounds fresh and creative. Anything that challenges our preconceptions and helps to shape the way we see the world.

In Shakespeare's play, Hamlet doesn't execute at pace—that's his tragedy. When he finds Claudius at prayer in Act 3, Hamlet flunks the opportunity to slay him and avenge his murdered father. He fears that Claudius's repentant words at the moment of death will deliver him undeservedly to heaven. Hamlet prefers to wait for a time when his uncle is "about some act/That has no relish of salvation in't."

By drawing out his revenge, Hamlet sets in motion a series of events that ultimately leads to his destruction—his procrastination gives the play its momentum. The focus of the drama becomes Hamlet's struggle to take on a role—that of avenger—for which he finds himself unequipped. That struggle is charted through a series of complex and intimate speeches in which a solitary Hamlet seeks answers to profound questions. Here, Shakespeare uses soliloquy—those confessional speeches direct to the audience—in a more sophisticated way than he had done before in his work, to the point where they become the play's pulsating heart.

In these speeches, Hamlet sometimes stumbles or hesitates, sometimes his language soars skyward. Sometimes exasperation intensifies into desperation. Sometimes we fear that his madness—the "antic disposition" adopted as part of his revenge plot—isn't just an act: perhaps he really has taken leave of his senses? The play becomes as much about Hamlet's state of mind as it is about the state of Denmark. We're never less than enthralled as he literally speaks his mind, drawing us into his world through layers of vivid metaphor. Hamlet's precise circumstances are unique—his family gives new meaning to the word dysfunctional—but, in essence, his dilemma is one we all recognize: the struggle to find a direction in life. Don't we sometimes feel bruised and outcast? Don't we wish we were more at ease with the world? Hamlet's fate touches us—that's why each generation takes this play to their hearts and why the character's speeches are lodged in our common psyche. In "To be, or not to be," Hamlet's most famous soliloquy, he argues that we tolerate the miseries of life only out of a fear that death might bring something worse:

Thus conscience does make cowards of us all;
And thus the native hue of resolution
Is sicklied o'er with the pale cast of thought,
And enterprises of great pith and moment
With this regard their currents turn awry,
And lose the name of action. (*Act 3, Scene 1*)

Through such frank soul-searching, Hamlet forges an intimate bond with the audience. And our relationship with him is all the stronger because it's only to us that he can speak so frankly. His father is dead and most of the people close to him have their own agendas. His mother is married to his father's murderer. His friends Rosencrantz and Guildenstern are sent to spy on him. His lover Ophelia has betrayed his trust by passing his letters on to her father. As the darkness closes in, he has only the audience to turn to:

we are his confidants and co-conspirators. The world through Hamlet's eyes is both disturbing and captivating. Shakespeare urges us to forget our everyday concerns and take an eviscerating look at life from a different perspective. He wants to remind us what it is to be human—as all great art does.

By contrast, the language coming out of most company boardrooms makes little effort to influence or convince. That's a mistake, because to succeed in business you need to sway people's opinions and build support for your goals. There will always be companies that use jargon deliberately to be obfuscatory or to unsettle, but those that aspire to better things should give more thought to how they communicate.

They should begin by using fresh, original and lively language. Too much of today's jargon is appropriate only for dry command or instruction. Instead, businesses should start a conversation with their employees, using informal and accessible language in a tone of voice that's right for the organization. But the challenge isn't just the words businesses choose, it is also the content of what they say. You can't sound interesting if you don't have a strong message, but when you strip away the jargon, so much of what you reveal is worthless: do people really need to be told the importance of doing things quickly? Besides, an order like that is no good if employees aren't sure what it is they need to do quickly or even why speed is necessary. Businesses shouldn't just describe what needs to be achieved, they should indicate the part people can play in achieving it.

That kind of clear message is particularly important at times of change, for instance with the arrival of a new boss. Director Michael Almereyda's film of *Hamlet*, with Ethan Hawke as the prince, sets the play in the world of business. By killing his brother, Claudius becomes the new CEO of Denmark Corporation—a hostile takeover if ever there was one. Claudius's confident face at press conferences, as speculation mounts of a bid from Fortinbras, contrasts with growing private paranoia. Video surveillance footage, intercepted emails and hidden microphones—Ophelia is sent by Claudius and Polonius to Hamlet wearing a concealed wire—create a perfect modern correlative for the paranoia that grips the court in Shakespeare's play. Even as the threat looms from outside, the state of Denmark turns in on itself, with tragic results.

At the end of the play, Fortinbras, the new king of Denmark, endorses Horatio's suggestion that the story of what happened should be told "lest more mischance/On plots and errors happen." Fortinbras recognizes the dangers of gossip and speculation, which inevitably fill the vacuum when the real picture is uncertain. As he takes up the crown, he wants to circulate a true account of the self-destruction of Claudius's court before rumours threaten his authority. Similarly, when companies don't communicate well—when they spew out jargon and fail to give a clear direction—their employees can be forgiven for making things up as they go along.

Businesses can learn a lot from the power of great narratives—after all, there are few better ways of seizing an audience's attention. Companies should tell a story of what they want to achieve. Instead of simply demanding a "step change" in performance, they should explain what that means in practice and collect examples that people can learn from.

Developing a compelling narrative for a business isn't an easy task. It forces companies to think about their priorities and what they really want from the people who work for them—all too often, jargon enables you to dodge these challenges with bland, catch-all statements. But there are good business reasons for communicating better. Employees who can see the journey ahead more clearly are likely to be more enthusiastic about it. When their role is well defined they can better concentrate their efforts. When they feel inspired by what the business has to say, they are more likely to be loyal. Most importantly, by banishing jargon you compel everyone in an organization to think more carefully about what they really mean. That should raise the standard of the conversation and translate into improved performance. Put simply, businesses can increase their chances of "executing at pace" if they ditch phrases like that one.

There are numerous challenges. Many business leaders are outstanding communicators in person. Few CEOs would be flattered by a comparison with Claudius, but witness the self-serving brilliance of his speech that opens the play's second scene: by managing the interpretation of recent events he secures the early days of his kingship. Often the trouble arises when business leaders have to put their thoughts down on paper. It's true that technology such as company television channels and podcasts give bosses more scope to address employees directly, but other mainstays of modern communications—such as email and intranet—rely on the written word. In general, business leaders need to be much better at written communications, much more fluent and engaging.

What they need is a writer in their closest team. Perhaps they're concerned that if someone else does the writing they won't sound like themselves. Truth is, a good writer can help you sound more like yourself—perhaps even a more eloquent version of you. They can bring your personality alive in the written word, where it is so often lost. And they can make you sound like you have a vision, not just a vision statement.

Indeed, one answer to many of the communications challenges that companies face is to put writers at the heart of the business. The fate of too many business writers is to skulk in the shadows at the periphery of an organization, rather like Hamlet in the court of Denmark. Instead, companies should embrace them. These writers should be commercially astute and strategically aware—just the kind of people that Shakespeare, the highly commercial playwright, investor and businessman, might applaud.

I have worked both as a writer in a company's communications team and as an agency copywriter serving corporate clients. I have helped airports to discuss noise pollution, accountancy firms to explain tax legislation, and engineering firms to boast efficiency improvements. I accept that jargon can possess its own deceptive poetry—indeed, I have sat through presentations in which buzzwords have been used with such fluency that the overall effect has been almost hypnotic. OK, so these presentations left no lasting impression, but they certainly sounded impressive and urgent at the time. In essence, though, buzzwords *are* noise pollution. It's our job as writers to resist jargon's dazzling allure—to step back from the brink—and help businesses to achieve the detachment that's necessary for effective communication.

In the world of politics, speechwriters and other communications specialists have long been part of the inner sanctum. Some would argue it shows the ascendancy of "spin," but it does underline the relationship between communication and execution: to get something done, you have to make your case convincingly. Indeed, there may be times when the message determines the policy, rather than vice versa.

Similarly, writers can help businesses to see how their story "plays" to an audience. And because good writing demands careful thought, writers can help businesses to join the dots: they can spot the gaps in the story and ensure you deliver a coherent and compelling strategy—whether to employees, customers or investors.

In other words, businesses should heed Hamlet's instructions to the actors he hires to perform "The Mousetrap," a play he hopes will expose Claudius's guilt. He directs them to pronounce the speech "trippingly on the tongue" and urges them "to suit the action to the word, the word to the action." That's in contrast to Claudius himself, who admits in the next scene that his repentant prayers aren't the words of a repentant man:

My words fly up, my thoughts remain below.
Words without thoughts never to heaven go.
(Act 3, Scene 3)

One of the themes of *Hamlet* is the relationship between thoughts, words and action. Businesses need to reach the point where communication isn't just the glitter on top, but where it begins to inform the way that they think and behave as an organization. Where a company better articulates what it wants to achieve—and so increases its chances of getting there.

Shakespeare's plays remind us what really matters in life, when less important things—such as a bad day at the office—threaten to preoccupy us. His highly charged dramas revolve around archetypal human experiences, helping us to make sense of the world and readying us for life's hurdles. But businesses can learn from these plays too. That's because Shakespeare shows the extraordinary potential of language as a galvanizing and inspiring force—even in Hamlet, a play about inaction.

Creative Partnerships

Emma Lawson on *Much Ado About Nothing*

Principal Actor: Henry Condell

Go on, "press me to death with wit"[1]

My favourite chocolate bar is a Mint Aero. It's so sharply sweet it gives me an anticipated, then instant intense visceral pleasure. Snap off a piece, pop it in the mouth, crunch through the bubbles, and wait for the sugar to rush to the brain. *Much Ado About Nothing* can have that effect on me, too.

The play's headspinning hit is its frictional double act, Beatrice and Benedick (not its more conventional lovers, Claudio and Hero, whose relationship is like an arduously chewy toffee that endangers my fillings). Like other memorable pairings, audiences keep coming back to watch these two scrap and squabble their way through events and into each other's arms. Alone Beatrice and Benedick would be funny, but they'd go largely unchallenged. The subtleties of their language—multiple meanings, metaphor pile-ups, preference for prose—might pass unnoticed, their opinions harden, their wit cease through lack of use. That's a future they narrowly escape. Instead, they meet and subject their audience to a barrage of verbal virtuosity and pratfall comedy that can't be matched by Shakespeare's other lovers. Why?

Situation, for starters. Neither has been washed up on the coast of a foreign land (*Twelfth Night*), they're not under

1 *Much Ado About Nothing*, edited by Claire McEachern, London, 2006, Act 3, Scene 1, 76.

any enchantment (*A Midsummer Night's Dream*), or in disguise (*As You Like It*), there's no feud between their families (*Romeo and Juliet*), neither is mad—real or feigned (*Hamlet*), and no one's trying to prevent them getting together (*Measure for Measure*) or pull them apart (*Othello*).

No. Here they are, thrown together after the successful conclusion of a battle, with all the attendant relief and high spirits that brings. The victors can turn their attention to gentler pursuits. And Claudio, Benedick's "new sworn brother,"[2] gets to it on line 154 of the first scene: "didst thou note the daughter of Signor Leonato?"[3] Unlike their Shakespearean cousins Viola and Orsino or Rosalind and Orlando for example, Beatrice and Benedick are free to express their opinions, are well liked, respected and supported; and they're equals. There's nothing to stop them treading the same primrose path of dalliance as Claudio and Hero—except themselves. And who are they? They're intelligent, witty and defensive, and they just can't resist being drawn into a "merry war"[4] against each other, and against the pervasive mood of love in the house.

Beatrice: *I had rather hear my dog bark at a crow, than a man swear he loves me.*[5]

Benedick: *Prove that ever I lose more blood with love than I will get again with drinking, pick out mine eyes with a ballad-maker's pen and hang me up at the door of a brothel-house for the sign of blind Cupid.*[6]

Signor Mountanto and Lady Disdain have thrown down their challenges—the fun's about to start.

Actors like Judi Dench, John Gielgud, Peggy Ashcroft and Derek Jacobi have been attracted to these roles, perhaps because of their combative, passionate, expressive qualities that are really only brought out through contact with each

---

2 *Much Ado About Nothing*, edited by Claire McEachern, London, 2006, Act 1, Scene 1, 68.
3 ibid., Act 1, Scene 1, 154–155.
4 ibid., Act 1, Scene 1, 58.
5 ibid., Act 1, Scene 1, 125–126.
6 ibid., Act 1, Scene 1, 233–236.

other. It's easy to conjure a picture of what rehearsals might be like as a Beatrice and a Benedick emerge through the efforts of the actors playing them. Of course these two actors wouldn't work alone—like Beatrice and Benedick who need a Don Pedro to bring them together, and a Messina audience to react to them, the actors have a director, a cast, an audience. But in their performance, on stage, they must bring Beatrice and Benedick to life. And these partnerships—Beatrice and Benedick, actor and actress—for me have the flavour of other creative relationships; those that produce books, short films, movies, patented products. All harness imagination to an end result. All can be thrilling to observe or be a part of.

I've talked to a few people who've had this experience. All of them described how different it was, working with another person. Neil, a writer, distinguished between the relatively smooth, known process of working by himself, and the "messy, enjoyable, less slick, and really unpredictable" time he had developing a project with a designer. And they were also clear about the relative rarity of "the real thing," the experience of intense creative connection. Anthony, a film editor who's been in the business for many years, said: "It's happened twice in my working life. I knew absolutely that it was happening at the time: you have to grab it and encourage the moment."

There's an indefinable, unscientific *something* that leads to a successful creative partnership. It spins around ideas like respect, a shared sense of humour, "getting on"—impulses that you can't make up. But, as with Beatrice and Benedick, if these feelings tangibly exist and connect two people, there are ways of encouraging a creative partnership into being. And this involves—spoken or not—some rules.

Beatrice and Benedick repulse and attract like a pair of magnets. As though they've walked past a mirror and instead of glimpsing themselves they've seen the other, they're intrigued, fascinated, irritated by this person who shares their language. There's no one else like it in *Much Ado*, no one who can cut and thrust and return the blows the way they do. And because of this bond, this impulsive engagement, they can't be anything other than themselves; a good place to start since "the basis of any creative relationship is being completely natural and allowing of the moment, being oneself at all times and never forcing a situation." Which is risky, unless there's a tacit agreement to be open, honest and accepting—then there's the "ability to say anything, however crazy and seemingly unrelated, and know that the discussion stays 'within the room.'"

But this isn't going to happen with just anyone. In the world of Messina, Benedick and Beatrice are seen even by themselves as entertainers ("jester"[7] and "fool"[8])—"We have been up and down to seek thee [Benedick], for we are high-proof melancholy and would fain have it beaten away. Wilt thou use thy wit?"[9] They bear out a recurrent thought: that it's rare to find a person who can both support and enhance another's creativity. However. Although Beatrice and Benedick recognize their affinity, they refuse to acknowledge it. They're habitually tussling, laying down challenges, pushing the other to new heights of absurdity. Or they're insisting to whoever will listen, with increasingly desperate intensity, that the single life is the one to have.

The tension between Beatrice and Benedick is hugely productive (for the audience it's the Aero effect—"When are they next on? What are they going to do next?"—the anticipated bam! of pleasure). The same kind of tension drives partnerships in the creative industries: "Pushing and allowing yourself to be pushed is all-important in a collaborative creative process," says Nic, a film cameraman. But he's found that, as with Shakespeare's couple, it's more likely to yield results if the participants are equals: "There's something important about being on the same level. Perhaps, like boxing, it makes the fights more exciting. If one person dominates over the other at every turn the process is a little staid."

Although some people I asked had found competitiveness useful as a way of encouraging each other, there was also the understanding, expressed by Anthony, that you have to "give up the sense of ownership. The ownership of ideas is extremely difficult to attribute and, if you want the partnership to continue, best left unclaimed." Neil agrees:

---

7 *Much Ado About Nothing*, edited by Claire McEachern, London, 2006, Act 2, Scene 1, 223.

8 ibid., Act 1, Scene 1, 37.

9 ibid., Act 5, Scene 1, 122–124.

"Give things away—let someone else play with your ideas—see what happens." And Nic adds that "it's a strange anomaly that I would want to do the best job I can for [the director] but that following her route on set won't always produce the best results in my department. There's a balance to be found between creating the best work as a whole and creating *my* best work, which may damage the work as a whole."

All this is about being ourselves, but not being self-centred: about sharing through communication. And to what end? To connect with an audience. No viewer/ listener/ reader/buyer, no point. Beatrice and Benedick's wit thrives on the to and fro of conversation—they need an audience. They have a willing one in Messina. Other characters on stage with them are silent witnesses to their skirmishes or straight men to their act. In the seats beyond is their other audience, laughing with pleasure at their fractious encounters, moved by their declarations of love, taking away lasting memories of subliminal moments when actors, words and watchers spark together.

The actor can't ignore the audience (they're out there ...), nor can the creative team working on a project. Imagination and originality without an outcome is not creativity (well, not according to the dictionary). And an outcome that's not matched to its intended recipients has failed in its purpose (and sometimes goes down in history, particularly if it's been expensive to produce). One of the world's great partnerships, that of John Hemmings and Henry Condell, had their audience very much in mind when they compiled the first collected edition of Shakespeare's plays: "To the great Variety of Readers ... It is now publique, & you will stand for your priviledges wee know: to read and censure. Do so, but buy it first."[10] Enough people bought and treasured the First Folio for around 230 to survive from a total of about 750.[11] Not bad for a book that's nearly 400 years old.

Each project has its limits and can be liberating for that, as Sara, a teacher, writer and ex-children's book editor, puts it: "I think constraints are vital in the creative process.

---

10 From the opening pages of the First Folio, A3.

11 Folio, where art thou?" by Paul Collins, September 2006, www.smithsonianmagazine.com.

Otherwise poetry would not exist." Nic is one half of a team that has produced several short films, and acknowledges the importance of remembering that at some point the creative conversation will have to be "born into a real world in which, ultimately, dozens of people will have to work in uncompromising surroundings to produce the final piece."

And it's not just the involvement of a larger team that checks ideas that were staggeringly brilliant in concept and are completely bonkers in reality. There're deadlines and budgets, and guidelines and formats. A successful creative partnership has an in-built "delete" button. Carina works with a colleague who "can make me feel creative by getting excited by my ideas while I play devil's advocate so that she doesn't get too carried away with ideas that are unrealistic." These limits are there for a reason: creative partnerships must always keep their audience in sight.

I'm not sure Beatrice and Benedick always do. It's the kind of thing that depends on the production you see, but there's a point at which they go too far and are in danger of going from a bubbly burst of Aero to a solid mass of turgid toffee.... Can they ever be civil to each other again? Chance steps in.

Don Pedro decides to undertake "one of Hercules' labours" and bring Beatrice and Benedick into a "mountain of affection"[12] for each other (note the hyperbole that goes hand-in-hand with any mention of these two). He and his accomplices intend to supplant Cupid: "his glory shall be ours, for we are the only love-gods."[13] What sport.

Beatrice and Benedick fall instantly—there's no prevarication, no hesitation. He even blatantly talks himself into it: "No, the world must be peopled."[14] Beatrice, meanwhile, like Benedick a confirmed proser amid lines and lines of iambic pentameter, breaks into verse:

And Benedick, love on, I will requite thee,
Taming my wild heart to thy loving hand.

12 *Much Ado About Nothing*, edited by Claire McEachern, London, 2006, Act 2, Scene 1, 336–338.
13 ibid., Act 2, Scene 1, 357.
14 ibid., Act 2, Scene 2, 233.

If thou dost love, my kindness shall incite thee
To bind our loves up in a holy band.[15]

Quite a change.

Chance is like the third person in a creative partnership. It is risk, happy accident, opportunity. And it won't happen if you try and force it. The *Collins Dictionary* defines chance as "the unknown and unpredictable element that causes something to happen in one way rather than another." Here's an example from a film editor's perspective. "I was working with a director I got on with really well," says Anthony. "We were at the 'first cut' stage where I assemble the film from miles of footage. The director was nervous about a particular scene because it was pivotal to the whole piece and he asked me to assemble it in a way that would use as much of the material as possible. The scene fell into four sections; I made four different versions of each section and then joined them all together. The result produced some extraordinary juxtapositions of thought and image, so much so that we kept the device and used it in the final film."

So what does Don Pedro's chance involvement in their affairs do to Beatrice and Benedick? It brings out in both a range of expression that's quite unexpected. While playfulness remains at the heart of their relationship, there's the introduction of a depth and plainness that were missing before.

Beatrice: *I love you with so much of my heart that none is left to protest.*
Benedick: *Come, bid me do anything for thee.*
Beatrice: *Kill Claudio.*
Benedick: *Ha, not for the wide world.*
Beatrice: *You kill me to deny it. Farewell.*[16]

For many, this is an intensely moving, shocking moment in the play, made so by its monosyllabic brevity—and hopefully the acting, too. This seriousness is an important development; it doesn't undercut Beatrice and Benedick's wit, it

15 *Much Ado About Nothing*, edited by Claire McEachern, London, 2006, Act 3, Scene 1, 111–114.
16 ibid., Act 4, Scene 1, 285–290.

softens it. The defences have dropped away. From this point in the play their responses will be better matched to the situations they find themselves in. There's a sense now that they can take more risks with their thoughts, try things out, make connections, explore, because they're not going to hurt each other. "Thou and I are too wise to love peaceably,"[17] says Benedick, meaning that they're too sharp-witted not to question things, but also perhaps that they know the value of a good debate.

They have, in other words, achieved the ideal circumstances in which a creative partnership will flourish. And it feels like this is a Shakespearean marriage that really will continue to develop and prosper beyond the bounds of the play.

Which is actually what happened to the people I talked to on this subject. Yes, all were pleased with the output from their creative partnerships, but what stood out was the pleasure they've experienced working with others, who become friends. And friendships can last well beyond jobs—which seems like a good place to end.

Random tips for really creative partnerships:

1. take risks
2. keep your imagination well fed
3. share your ideas
4. go for the Aero moments (bam!)
5. stay open
6. exercise your right to "delete" …

… and don't forget your audience.

17 *Much Ado About Nothing*, edited by Claire McEachern, London, 2006, Act 5, Scene 2, 67.

Fifteen Scenes from an Imaginary Workshop

Laura Forman on *Titus Andronicus*

Principal Actor: William Sly

Scene I, 1.58 PM

My real name doesn't matter any more. I have become Willow Sly.

Click … and twist. A good luck kiss from my Nars lipstick in this season's Tamango and it's bye-bye to "me time" for the next three hours. One last look in the mirror and I head back to the room where I'll be running the workshop.

It's too small even for the handful of people who are coming. There's nothing worse than a tiny space—the air acquires top notes of corporate coffee on a musky base of working lunch. The room itches with hard-wearing nylon carpet in swirls of technicolor vomit shades. At least the chairs look quite comfortable.

The suburb this office is in is sprawling so fast it's probably going to give the M25 freeway stretchmarks. The company is newly formed, a merger between Vidian and ProSight. Even though it would sound more elegant the other way around, they've called it ProSight Vidian. No one can argue with alphabetical order. It doesn't actually matter that much to me what they do, but I mmm-ed and ah-ed my way through a 40-minute explanation. I even took some notes. It pays, in every sense, to show willing.

I'm such a pitch-bitch these days. The bit I like best is when I've got them dangling on the end of a twitching phone line. I love reeling them in with promises of curing the ills of modern working life in a half-day session. In reality, it's more about unplugging people. Rediscovering the world beyond the inbox. Sometimes that's enough. The thing about being an actor is knowing when you're putting on a show for yourself. These companies seem to go for the fact that I was once on stage. Still should be, really. But I let those reviews matter to me. A few flimsy bits of newsprint ruined everything. The limelight turned into a searchlight and my confidence disappeared. They don't need to know that, though. Make it sound like a deliberate career change and everyone's happy.

Scene II, 2.20 PM

My Apple's fired up and connected to the projector, leggy flipcharts poised. Workbooks and pencils wait on every chair. They're printed with *Willow Sly: Trainer* and my number in matt black, or *Burlesque Kohl* as they called it at the chi-chi bespoke stationery shop.

Scene III, 2.26 PM

"Willow ..."

He says my name as he enters the room and puts his hand out at the same time, leaving him a few paces to cover before we can make contact. The handshake tallies up with the voice, though, the one I know from those briefing chats on the phone. It's Tony and his reassuringly easy brand of businesslike bonhomie. Not fat, not thin, he's probably early forties or so.

"Got everything you need?" he asks, with the kind of expression that makes me think he actually would scurry round the building rounding up extra marker pens if I needed him to.

"Yes, yes. All raring to go."

"Great.... Well, I came along a few minutes early to give you a heads-up—it's not been plain sailing since the merger ..."

"Oh really? Feathers flying then?"

"That's one way of putting it. The Vidian guys are so much more buttoned-up than us. They're wanting us to adopt their processes, their style, their way of doing things. But ProSight's always tried to have the human touch."

"Yes, nimble and friendly." I playback his favourite phrase.

"But we're looking forward to the day, Willow. It's so important for us to get fresh perspectives in this time of flux."

This bonhomie is good stuff. The man's a talking management textbook but just twinkly enough to get away with it. Wedding ring. Dammit.

"How did the trip to the Globe go?"

"Ah, OK … I was glad no one fainted," says Tony. "I hadn't bargained for that in the risk assessment forms. Human Resources would've had something to say about it. Especially with all the vegetarians in the group."

Scene IV, 2.30 PM

I am all smiles, confident posture and expansive gestures as the herd settles itself.

"Right. Hello and welcome to the Titus Andronicus course from my award-winning series *Making Shakespeare Work For You*. You'll see from the agenda in your workbook we have a busy day ahead. Tony organized a trip to the Globe for you all to watch the play. From experience, I know that these courses are so much more valuable if you're familiar with the themes. Did everyone make it along to that?"

Everyone but one, it seems. And he's the archetypal legs-and-arms-crossed disenchanted workshop attendee. Nothing will impress him so I may as well concentrate on the others.

"Not to worry, Greg. There's a summary of the plot in your workbook. It's no walk in the park, of course, but even Quentin Tarantino would be hard pushed to squeeze more violence into a couple of hours. We've got a returning hero, executive skullduggery, a forced marriage, child sacrifice, rape and mutilation, double-crossing, wrongful arrest, more mutilation, an illicit pregnancy and, to cap it all, the baddies get baked in a pie and eaten by their mother."

Scene V, 3.30 PM

An hour in and we've refreshed memories by putting the key scenes of the play in order and discussed the experience of watching it in the, often very bloody, flesh. Michelle, who looks well used to raising temperatures at the water cooler, was, like, totally grossed out. Shantha, a much shrewder-looking cookie, chips in: "I went to the Japanese production in Stratford and it was really interesting to compare the stylized portrayal of violence with the stage-blood realism of the Globe production."

Quite so. I better nip this in the bud. "Of course, Peter Brook's 1955 production also used red ribbons to represent blood. It's not *such* a new idea."

"Yes, I know," replies Shantha. "But apparently Vivien Leigh was remarkable as Lavinia."

"I'm thrilled you're taking such an interest."

"*Titus* was one of the texts for my Masters."

Scene VI, 3.32 PM

I decide it's time to introduce an idea that struck me when I was planning this day. The spa was keeping me on hold while I was trying to book a massage appointment so I had plenty of time to think it through, and the looped whalesong proved stimulating. When Titus returns to Rome with a clutch of Goth prisoners, it looks as if he's liquidated their assets on the battlefield—the Romans have acquired the Goths. But then the marriage of Tamora, the Queen of Goths, to the newly appointed Roman emperor gives her an executive role on the board. Older than her toy-boy emperor, she's clever enough to bow and scrape to the bigwigs, making it look as if she's thrilled to be a Roman, all the while plotting how to get back at them. I'd hoped the group would lap this up, feeling the parallels with the Vidian ProSight merger, but they won't spill the beans. It often happens when you have someone, twinklesome though he is, as senior as Tony in the room. Better go for a more concrete approach.

Scene VII, 3.37 PM

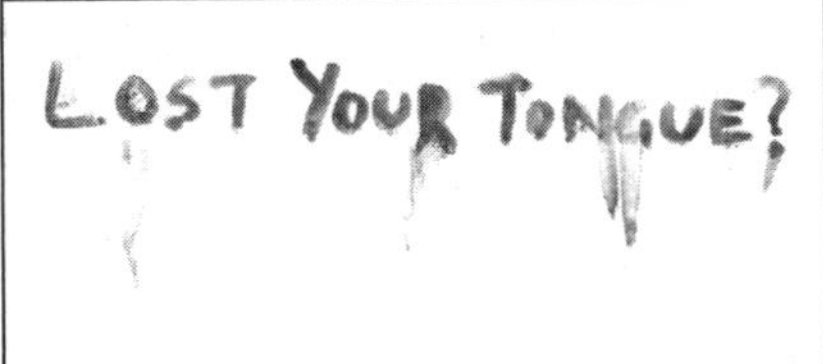

It does the soul good to indulge in handicrafts now and again. I made that slide myself, smearing the words in fake blood and even managing to get a few clot-like globs to stick. I'm almost scared it will gross Michelle out more than the play. But this is the theme for the rest of the day. I'd bet a Diptyque scented candle that the first image anyone thinks of in connection with *Titus Andronicus* is Lavinia. Her new husband killed in front of her, she wanders in the woods after being raped and having had her hands and tongue butchered.

Scene VIII, 4.02 PM

"So if we agr ee Vidian ProSight has, like Lavinia, got some severe communication issues, what can we do about it? Any bright ideas?"

The group is suddenly mute. There's been plenty of jousting between the Vidian and ProSight camps about their respective styles of communication. Vidian are campaigning for what they see as "standards," ProSight railing against being pushed to communicate more formally. Memos in triplicate, that kind of nonsense. I'm not sure where Vidian have been while the tone of voice revolution's been going on. Even banks sound as if they're next to you in the hot tub these days. I get the group to bring out the examples of effective communication they were briefed to bring along. Not a big surprise that they've all picked warm and engaging ads and leaflets. I'm sure we can win Vidian round.

Scene IX, 4.04 PM

I trawl the room for eyeballs and drag the harvest behind me as I catwalk glide to the Apple. I managed to squeeze a little homework in before the session and have drawn up pros and cons of the Vidian and ProSight positions. I display them with a flourish.

"Willow, I'm not entirely comfortable with anything based on comparisons between our corporate situation and poor Lavinia," says Shantha.

I'm fluent enough in Corporatese to know what this means. She hates me.

"Shantha. This workshop is exactly the right arena to explore such views. But it's time for a break now. Let's regroup in ten minutes or so."

Scene X, 4.09 PM

"The session's going well." Important to make that a statement, not a question. Tony and I are approaching this break with more relish than strictly appropriate. All kinds of elaborate behaviours over who gets the last chocolate biscuit. I can scarcely admit it'll be the first to pass my lips in four and a half years.

"You're certainly introducing some ideas that are new to us. Time and space to evaluate our situation is always useful. We may even be making steps toward a compromise between the Vidian and ProSight positions," he confirms.

And steps toward some compromising positions for the two of us, if I'm not mistaken.

"Willow is such an unusual name," he volunteers, venturing outside his managerial vocabulary.

"Thanks," I purr. "It's my stage name, of course. I had to rechristen myself when I was applying for my Equity card."

"What inspired it?"

"William Sly was a member of Shakespeare's company. I thought it would be fun to inhabit an identity with that kind of history."

"And what's your real name?"

"Oh, these days I only reveal that to people I know *very* well, Tony ..."

I make a mental note to text tonight's Lukewarm Date and postpone our dinner until further notice.

Scene XI, 4.16 PM

"So, we've looked at ProSight Vidian's communication issues on a macro scale. Now I'd like to zoom in and think about techniques that will help you, as individuals, talk your way to the top."

People love to focus on themselves. I include myself in that, of course. Workshop atmospheres always brighten when there's an obvious answer to the background drone of "What's in it for me?"

"Let's help you find, or rediscover, your tongue and make work more, ah, satisfying. Going back to an early scene, let's imagine how Tamora might influence her new husband, the Emperor."

I choose Michelle and Greg to do some role play. I worry Michelle will be too smug at being picked to play the sexy queen to engage with the exercise. But she's surprisingly good.

"Excellent work, guys. Does anyone have any observations about Greg's responses to Michelle?"

There's a muttering about last year's Christmas party. I develop selective deafness and invite more serious comment with a miraculously schoolmarmish eyebrow manoeuvre.

"He was more prepared to listen once she'd taken the time to get him to trust her," someone suggests.

"Exactly, er …" I can't quite see their name badge.

Scene XII, 5.03 PM

We're on the home straight. I'm helping the group explore the, frankly, essential art of negotiation. I've already introduced my theory of Preparing the Ground for the Big Ask. We're working on the first part now. I've paired everyone up and am forcing them to lavish each other with convincing, yet subtle, compliments. As the group's an odd number, I'm making up a pair. In an unusual moment of conscientiousness, I picked Shantha over Tony.

She stands in front of me, searching for something to say.

"Your, uh, boots are very unusual."

I think the other pairs are getting on fine, though. It's time for them to step up a gear and practise asking for the fruits of office life: holidays, pay rises, a desk by the window, time and a half for overtime.

Scene XIII, 5.20 PM

People are sneaking looks at their watches. I feel the same.

Scene XIV, 5.24 PM

I've just a few minutes spare for a final chat and the inevitable feedback forms. The room and, I'm sure, the grey fuzzy-felt cubicles beyond can't wait to eject their daytime occupants and settle down to twilight standby mode. I wonder what will be said at dinner tables tonight.

It's all progressing innocuously enough. Almost too good to be true.

"But Willow, don't you think the real point is that Shakespeare made so many observations about what it is to be human that he's relevant to any aspect of life, including business?"

"That's all we have time for today. Thanks everyone!"

Scene XV, 5.34 PM

Tony's asked me to meet him in his office when I've got my things together. I gather up the left-behind pencils with the usual sense of amazement that people can bear not to take such design icons home with them. Or at least to their desks.

Back to the bathroom with its overwhelming accumulation of toxic lemon sherbet-scented air freshener. I'm just about to flush when I hear people come in.

"She wasn't really open to conversation, though. Whenever I made a point, she made some excuse and moved us on."

It's Shantha.

"Yeah but it was alright though. I mean that role-play session was quite funny. I might have lunch with Greg tomorrow. Before I ask Tony for a pay rise."

And Michelle. Go girl!

"Well, she seems like some has-been actress who wants to think that all the office is a stage."

They're bantering to each other from adjacent cubicles.

I am frozen in my own. I wait—an anonymous and assumed constipated occupant—through their hairbrushing and lip glossing and see you tomorrowing.

The office is a wilderness of tigers. I've lost the heart, or something along those lines, for Tony now. I evaporate into the evening, wondering what time he'll give up and go home.

Mass Storytelling and the Power of Advertising

Liz Holt on *The Merchant of Venice*

Principal Actor: Richard Cowley

Imagine you are six years old. Imagine you're completely and utterly lost in a story. Your imagination has so powerfully transported you to another world that you're not even aware that you're holding a book and turning the pages.

But something calls you back from that place. In two thumps of your heart you're aware of the book and the ink-stained school desk under your hands. Quick as a wink, you look up. But it's not your classmates around you and not your class teacher glaring at you. You have been so enchanted that you weren't aware of your own class leaving the room and friends yanking your grey woollen sweater, trying to get your attention.

A few kids titter. Flushed, you mumble some words, grab your bag and stumble out of the classroom.

This happened to me at Moss Hey Junior School. And in that moment I realized two things: first, stories were powerful, even dangerous; second, I was a story junkie. I was hooked.

I grew up with *Anne of Green Gables*, Stig from the dump, Charlie and his chocolate factory, *The Iron Man*, *The Little Prince* on the moon. I cuddled my own *Velveteen Rabbit*. I wanted to change my name to tragic and beautiful Beth from *Little Women* (then, secretly, was delighted to be called Lizzie when I first encountered the tall, dark mysterious Darcy stereotype). Something about stories, about narrative, gripped me.

And I'm not alone in this. Tim Byrne—now, interestingly, a book cover designer—confesses to story-influenced thinking when he was seven. He stood amid wild flowers and lush grass beneath a glittering sky with his mate Tiff and they held out their hands, closed their eyes and called out "Aslan! Aslan! Aslan!" For a minute or two, they believed a door would magically appear and, like Eustace and Jill, they would walk into Narnia.

As a teenager, stories hit harder and bit deeper. I was appalled and thrilled that Shylock in *The Merchant of Venice* demanded a pound of Antonio's flesh. Shylock's blood thirst for vengeance, fuelled by prejudice, was my first awakening to character-driven action. I started to understand the power of characters drawn with psychological insight. I also remember the fury of others at the (apparent) anti-Semitism of the play.

I loved the ability of words to make you want to climb into yet another character's head, another life, another world. This love propelled me into advertising, working as a copywriter ever since.

The best TV commercials are mini stories. All the big brands down the decades—Bacardi, Guinness, Levi's, Bisto, Gold Blend, Smash and so on—use stories in this world of relatively homogenous products in the hope of creating a point of difference.

So what can *The Merchant of Venice* teach us? The title alludes to business but little commercial wheeling and dealing takes place, and the passive "*I know not why I am so sad*" Antonio is untypical of the proactive Venetian entrepreneurs. Like an English privateer, Bassanio's adventurous pursuit (at almost all costs) of the wealthy Portia, turns Antonio into a venture capitalist. From the gold, silver and lead caskets' storyline (a suitor's choice determined who Portia should marry), we have the wisdom of "*all that glisters is not gold.*" Like so many phrases that Shakespeare created, this articulates emotional intelligence and has entered our language.

Yet it's the intrinsic power of the story as a whole that, like all great stories, is the most profound and probably unconscious influence upon business writers today.

To watch the story acted on stage, Elizabethans rowed across the stinking, heaving River Thames and endured several hours on hard seats or standing in the thrashing rain in the pit. All simply to feel bewitched by the play. They chose to pay a penny for this experience instead of watching bear-baiting, cock-fighting, or disappearing into a tavern or brothel. Audiences were often over a thousand strong: for the first time stories became mass entertainment in Britain. And Shakespeare, together with Marlowe, Jonson, Webster, Fletcher and Middleton, made a living.

Shakespeare cast his spells through convincing characters and powerful plotlines. He wrote *The Merchant* following the success of Marlowe's *The Jew of Malta*, weaving together plots and themes from other stories: Ser Giovanni's *Il Pecorone* for the basic plot; the Indian Sanskrit epic *Mahabharata* for the flesh-bond story; *Gesta romanorum* for the casket story.

The character of Shylock is arguably and untypically the play's only character with true psychological depth, and the ideal anti-comedic character who blocks the action of the play. Unlike the malevolent Malvolio in *Twelfth Night*, Shylock is cast as one of life's outsiders simply by birth, reflecting the prevalent anti-Semitism of the time. Because he is Jewish, he is spat upon by Antonio and others, is forced to live in a ghetto and is permitted to earn a living in few ways, one of which was usury. And for this he is despised.

Through Shylock, Shakespeare demonstrates what happens when human beings are pushed to extremes; he displays all the monomania that follows isolation and persecution. He is a tragic character, marking a turning point in Shakespeare's writing toward the great tragedies to come.

Two critical factors elicit our sympathy for Shylock. He learns that his daughter Jessica has run away with his jewels (Act 3, Scene 1) minutes before he discovers that Antonio's ships are lost. Next, he utters this highly emotive speech:

> *Hath not a Jew eyes? Hath not a Jew hands, organs, dimensions, senses, affections, passions; fed with the same food, hurt with the same weapons; subject to the same diseases, healed by the same means, warmed and cooled by the same winter and summer, as a Christian is? If you*

prick us, do we not bleed? If you tickle us, do we not laugh? If you poison us, do we not die? And if you wrong us, shall we not take revenge? If we are like you in the rest, we will resemble you in that. If a Jew wrong a Christian, what is his humility? Revenge. If a Christian wrong a Jew, what should his sufferance be by Christian example? Why revenge.

He then proceeds to take this one-off opportunity to assert himself.

Shakespeare also set Shylock in Venice—a place considered to be of dubious morality. Other characters in the play are hardly free of judgement, such as Jessica. Even the heroine Portia devises the cruel punishment that Shylock must forsake his religion and therefore his identity.

Yet we are presented with Shylock's monstrous desire to remove and weigh Antonio's flesh—the epitome of calculated murder. John Keats described this type of dramatic tension as Shakespeare's "negative capability"—his genius in taking a mass of conflicting notions and using the ensuing conflict to provide the drama.

Shylock is the outsider—stereotypically, since the earliest tales were spoken around fires, the one blamed for all ills. The bogey. The monster. The scapegoat. The Jungian projected shadow self.

Perhaps Shakespeare portrayed this outsider with such sympathy because at some level he, too, shared a sense of isolation. In Elizabethan and therefore firmly Protestant England, his parents were quietly Catholic. Nobody knows whether he shared his parents' convictions. But at a time when people were beheaded for less, when every play was censored by the Master of Revels, when theatres were regularly shut down if threatening views were perceived, Shakespeare was clearly unable to write about the Protestant–Catholic troubles. Yet in *The Merchant* he portrays someone who is an outsider due to his religion, conveniently setting it in a different country.

Plays had to be politically expedient; the power of stories was feared. Today in many countries, writers of all types still live in fear for telling stories in all their forms.

Stories are feared for their power—but why are they powerful?

As readers, listeners and viewers, we almost compulsively seek the experience of leaving our own reality to travel along with the story and feel somehow altered when we return. In fact, if some emotional or rational shift doesn't take place, we feel dissatisfied, as though the story hasn't "worked."

All of us tell stories, all the time. Whether that's beside the water cooler, in the bar, over the backyard fence, in the boardroom, in the press, in debating chambers, in the making of history. There's something fundamentally human about constructing meaning by connecting one event to another in a narrative; we make sense of life through stories.

But why?

As we absorb a story, we unconsciously play out the reality of our own life in a different context, as if the distance helps us to interpret life in a new way. So we don't just find stories entertaining or uplifting or exciting or frightening or whatever—at a subconscious level we find them helpful.

We are living stories with a beginning, middle and end. Our life is a journey, a staggering metaphorical passage through time. As Carl Jung writes, at the most primitive level it's a journey of survival from childhood through adolescence to adulthood, when we can reproduce and ensure the continuation of our own species. Stories could be archetypes: models of development that guide us as we move through our journey. It's as if we are programmed to deliver stories to each other. Through stories we are unconsciously encouraged to overcome the physical and psychological challenges we face; stories resonate powerfully within our subconscious.

Christopher Booker identifies a nucleus of situations and figures at the heart of all stories across all cultures in his book *The Seven Basic Plots*:

> *All kinds of story, however profound or however trivial, ultimately spring from the same source, are shaped around the same basic patterns and are governed by the same universal rules.*

Despite the darkness and ambiguity of the play, *The Merchant of Venice* has always been classed as a comedy because a series of situations are resolved which bring about the reconciliation of the two central couples, Bassanio to Portia and Nerissa to Gratiano.

Booker said that, "the essence of Comedy is always that some redeeming truth has to be brought out from shadows into the light." Comedy's distinguishing feature is the movement from feelings of winter to summer, from shadow to light, from incompletion to wholeness. A key character or event brings self-revelation and fulfilment and greater self-knowledge so that the protagonist passes to the next stage of maturity. The premise of the resolution, according to the genre, is that discovering who you really are becomes a pre-condition to living happily ever after.

It's difficult to identify the protagonist in *The Merchant*. If it is Shylock, this looks like satire; and not, if the protagonist is Bassanio. Neither Portia nor Antonio travels on a sufficiently complex journey to qualify as the protagonist. So because Shylock is the character with the strongest psychological depth and therefore most likely to be the protagonist, this does point to elements of satire within the play.

This is consistent with the common view that Shakespeare was never didactic. He holds the "truth" lightly and holds more firmly to mystery and ambiguity. Perhaps in this way he pre-dates postmodernism. Perhaps it's another reason why his plays have such resonance today.

However the protagonist issue is resolved and despite the moral tension surrounding Shylock, the play does conclude with a sense of resolution and optimism that has been created by the romantic reconciliations.

Exploring the power of story—and therefore Shakespeare's greatest influence upon us today—the premise in comedy that deeper self-discovery leads to happy-ever-after is an archetype that "speaks" to us in a way that bypasses our conscious mind. This could be why a sense of resolution can literally feel so satisfying and cause an emotional shift.

Most stories have this sense of brightening and resolution, even if they don't use overt humour and therefore can be categorized as comedy. And most TV commercials fall firmly into this category.

Why is advertising so successful in influencing our behaviour—why can it be so powerful? Is it just peer pressure, the collective ego at work? Even then, something must spark a new consensus within a peer group.

Perhaps its power lies in the way that the character or event that creates the satisfying story resolution is substituted with a brand. This is the case even when the brand is subtly epitomized by a character.

The brand changes the feeling of winter to summer, shadow to light, problem to solution, incompletion to wholeness.

This profound story archetype influences us powerfully in our subconscious. It connects with the part of us that is programmed to receive and be influenced by stories.

So despite the fact that at a conscious level we may not believe that a certain brand can make us more fulfilled, more mature, more whole, happier and more attractive, at a deeply unconscious level something else is taking place. If we are in the target audience for the commercial, the brand may be resonating very strongly within, creating a feeling of need for this brand that will deliver us into wholeness, completion and satisfaction.

In the process of coming to this conclusion, I asked lots of people which TV commercials they felt worked the best: Tango "Orange guy," "Blackcurrant;" Orange "Dancing couple" and "Black out" set in Manhattan; Gold Blend; Kwik-Fit; Lynx; Carling Black Label "Laundrette" and "Dambusters;" Pot Noodle "Miners;" Typhoo "Chimps;" Honda "Diesel;" Warburtons "Bread tree;" Guinness "Dancing man;" British Rail "Sighing chess pieces;" Nationwide "Brand new customers only;" Frazzles with Freddy Jones as the wolf. The public information films of the 1970s. Watch the ads on and on, and see how in their story structure they all substitute the redeeming character or event with a brand. Even when they are more dissonant and avant-garde.

If Sony is successful, by 2020 there'll be no more TV screens. Instead, we'll all be watching moving holograms in our living rooms, just like a mini stage. Everything—from advertising to the new Interactive Storytelling—will be communicated through a medium we don't yet know. In comparison to the mass entertainment of today, it will be more like a play … infinitely more dialogue-based. On this new stage, the focus will be upon the same elements—

character-driven, believable action—that make Shakespeare's stories so compelling. And perhaps, alarmingly, the hidden, unconscious universal story archetypes will be even easier to exploit.

Acknowledgements
Many thanks to Professor David Salter at Edinburgh University, screenwriter Mark Grindell, author Vivian French, Paul Mason, Ken Dixon, Suneel Gopal, Jo Scobie, Tim Byrne, David Garnder, Sarah Sinclair, Marie Storrar, Dan Frydman, Derek Sneddon, Ross Laurie, Zane Radcliffe, Edward Longbottom and Andy McGregor.

Fortune's Fool: Boom and Bust in Ancient Athens

Robert Mighall on *Timon of Athens*

Principal Actor: John Lowin

Timon of Athens is possibly Shakespeare's least read, least produced and most unusual play. Even the professional Shakespeareans I consulted claimed to have read it only once, and then in their distant pasts. There are doubts over its authorship (it is possibly a collaboration with Thomas Middleton); whether it is even properly finished; how to classify it; or that it was ever performed at all. It is a very short play. There are very few major characters, a rather half-hearted sub-plot, and the action (that is mostly dialogue) takes place over about ten days. Finding I'd been given the runt of the litter, I decided to give it extra love. But with *Timon* that word seems peculiarly inappropriate. If Shakespeare's hand wasn't wholly in it, neither, evidently, was his heart. His spleen perhaps. Even without the gore of *Titus*, the body count of *Macbeth*, or the melancholia of *Hamlet*, it leaves you with a very bleak impression of humanity. Timon's fall is swift, sharp and absolute, with little time to adjust to his change in fortunes, and with few straws of comfort to clutch at in the flood of misanthropy that engulfs the second half.

And yet, you don't have to dress the players in Armani or Hackett to see the play's direct relevance to modern business. For perhaps more than any in the canon, it is almost exclusively about the pursuit and management of finances. An economic tragedy in many senses. Spare, stark and stripped to the bone, and relentlessly materialist in the picture it paints of mankind's motivations.

Given its obscurity, I had better provide a quick plot synopsis. Timon is a rich citizen of Athens, who has a reputation for generosity, of which those whom he calls "friends" take full advantage. In the first act we see him bail out a friend from prison, finance a servant's wedding, and we hear the open-handed, open-hearted friend to man wax eloquent on the pleasures of giving: "We are born to do benefits. And what better or properer can we call our own than the riches of our friends" (Act 1, Scene 2, 99–101).[1] He backs this up by showering his guests with gifts. His only apparent return is flattery, which the toadies who buzz round him freely squander on him. Words cost nothing.

Act 2 immediately reveals that Timon is as deluded in the estimation of his friends as he is in his resources. His numerous debts are called in, and when Timon confidently calls on those he has supported or spoilt over the years, he returns bearing nothing but excuses. Timon rages against the ingratitude of his fair-weather friends, and invites them to a mock banquet where he serves up stones, hot water and hotter invective. He retires to a cave in the forests outside Athens, as confirmed in misanthropy as he was once in his philanthropy.

Timon will to the woods, where he shall find
Th' unkindest beast more kinder than mankind.
The gods confound—hear me, you good gods all—
Th' Athenians both within and out that wall.
And grant, as Timon grows, his hate may grow
To the whole race of mankind, high and low.
Amen.

(*Act 4, Scene 1, 35–41*)

Timon of Athens is a sort of *Christmas Carol* in reverse. Small wonder it is not to everyone's tastes. Lear rages, but eventually finds redemption; Hamlet swipes and snipes at humanity, but in time accepts his destiny and proves himself most princely. Timon dies offstage, broken by the world's

1 *Timon of Athens*, G. R. Hibberd (ed.) London: Penguin, 2005. All further references to the text are from this Penguin edition.

ingratitude. All passion, invective and fortune spent. His self-penned epitaph indicates no possible let-up in hostilities:

Here lies a wretched corse, of wretched soul bereft.
... A plague consume you wicked caitiffs left!
Here lie I Timon, who alive all living me did hate.
Pass by and curse thy fill, but pass and stay not here thy gait.
(Act 5, Scene 4, 70–75).

Punk rock, ancient Athenian style. At one point he takes to hurling stones with his insults, thus completing the picture of all-consuming nihilism that defines his new incarnation.

A fine punk, but perhaps a lousy tragic hero. Convention dictated that an identifiable flaw should explain a tragic hero's downfall. Lear has his blindness, Macbeth has his overreaching ambition (not to mention his wife), Othello his jealousy, Hamlet introspective inertia. What is Timon's flaw? His faithful steward, Flavius, offers his own interpretation:

Poor honest lord, brought low by his own heart,
Undone by goodness! Strange, unusual blood,
When man's worst sin is he does too much good ...
Rich only to be wretched, thy great fortunes
Are made thy chief afflictions ...
(Act 4, Scene 2, 37–45)

Such sentimentality doesn't really wash in the Aristotelian tragic world, which demands a proper human failing to pin the blame on. But it works within the world the play depicts: where trust looks more like naivety, generosity bad financial management, and where Timon's determination to spread happiness through largesse is countered by a reluctance to heed the counsel offered by his steward. There were numerous "profit warnings" before the swift collapse ensued:

O my good lord,
At many times I brought in my accounts,
Laid them before you. You would throw them off,
And say you found them in mine honesty.
... If you [now] suspect my husbandry of falsehood,
Call me before th' exactest auditors,
And set me on the proof.
(Act 2, Scene 2, 138–162)

From a business point of view Timon's flaws are manifest, and would be dealt with mercilessly in the pages of the *Financial Times*. While you'd have a job to find a modern business person "undone by goodness," there are countless examples of false financial confidences, bubbles inflated by hot air and "value" puffed by mere perceptions. Perception is the mainstay of the markets, where corporations and their dependent retinue can tumble as swiftly and absolutely as Timon. Perhaps *Timon* ought to be essential reading alongside Sarbanes-Oxley in today's corporate world. It is a tragedy that points directly and insistently toward the financial sphere, encouraging us to assess Timon's "fortunes" (in both senses) in the light of how they are managed.

It is by exploring the different meanings of the idea of fortune that Shakespeare's play provides a service to the modern business world. Here we see this world beginning to turn, and turn into a shape we recognize today.

"Fortune" both with and without initial capitals, appears repeatedly throughout the play. In the opening scene it is introduced in its traditional shape as the Roman goddess Fortuna—the personification of luck, and the deity who dispensed it. The Poet describes an oily ode he has penned to Timon:

I have upon a high and pleasant hill
Feigned Fortune to be throned. The base o'the' mount
Is ranked with all deserts, all kinds of natures,
That labour on the bosom of this sphere
To propagate their states. Amongst them all
Whose eyes are on this sovereign lady fixed
One do I personate of Lord Timon's frame,
Whom Fortune with her ivory hand wafts to her …
(Act 1, Scene 1, 67–74)

This blind and fickle goddess, usually depicted with her wheel, was a standard allegorical device up to the late Middle Ages. It reminded people not to put too much store in earthly advancement, as what Fortune can bestow she can so easily take away. If some are at the zenith of her wheel, then others must be below—some hoping to rise, others falling from an earlier eminence. When Kent finds himself in the stocks in *King Lear*, he has reached his nadir, and appeals to the goddess: "Fortune, good night: smile once more: turn thy wheel!" The scheming Edmond in the same play declares, "The younger rises when the old doth fall," when he plots against his father and brother. But later concedes that, "The wheel has come full circle. I am here," when he is vanquished by his brother Edgar.

Timon is bound fast to this wheel, that turns at breathtaking speed in the play. This is anticipated by the Poet, who completes his allegory:

When Fortune in her shift and change of mood
Spurns down her late beloved, all his dependants,
Which laboured after him to the mountain's top
Even on their knees and hands, let him fall down,
Not one accompanying his declining foot.
(Act 1, Scene 1, 87–91)

This provides a form of prologue to the play, suggesting that Fortune rather than any individual flaw is responsible for Timon's fall. We only see Timon occupy the extremes of her wheel. As Apematus tells Timon: "The middle of humanity thou never knewest, but the extremity of both ends" (Act 4, Scene 3, 302). He deals only in absolutes, and is self-conscious about his adoption of his new role, declaring: "I am Misanthropos, and hate mankind" (Act 4, Scene 3, 54). He becomes a type, and acts his new part to the hilt. Nor does he display any of the introspection or character "development" that we look for in Shakespeare's major tragedies. There are no soliloquies. When he speaks alone it is to vent his fury and call down vengeance on ungrateful mankind.

There is one brief moment of recognition before Timon descends into raving misanthropy when he acknowledges that, "Unwisely, not ignobly, have I given," again suggesting that mismanagement rather than any moral failing accounts for his situation. Denied psychological depth and a defining moral flaw, we have to look elsewhere for meaning: to external factors, and the ways and values of the social world the play depicts. A world, that, if taken at face value, does indeed appear to turn entirely according to the dictates of "fortune." But this time without an initial capital, without her wheel, and represented by the idol that has usurped the goddess's authority. As Timon rages:

Gold? Yellow, glittering, precious gold?
... Thus much of this will make
Black white, foul fair, wrong right,
Base noble, old young, coward valiant.
... This yellow slave
Will knit and break religions, bless th'accursed,
Make leprosy adored, place thieves,
And give them title, knee and approbation,
With senators on the bench.

(*Act 4, Scene 3, 26–36*)

It is gold rather than Fortune that now effects reversals in fortune and state. A fortune can now achieve what the goddess once blindly bestowed. And it is the more narrow financial sense of the word that gains authority as the play proceeds. A narrowing that closely matches the historical "fortunes" of the word itself. The *Oxford English Dictionary* shows that the sense of the word as "an ample stock of wealth" was emergent at the time of the play. It cites its first use from 1596, a mere nine years before *Timon* was (probably) written. The meaning was new, and Shakespeare was exploring its ramifications.

From a personification of luck (good or bad), the term has in time come to refer exclusively to the accumulation of material wealth. Fortunes are made (and lost) on Wall Street through investments in Fortune 500 companies. Read about them and their figureheads in *Fortune* magazine. Emulate these figures and carve out your own fortune. The main difference between this and the earlier idea of Fortune, is the greater role given to human agency in the process. While we might claim an aristocrat was fortunate in his birth, we are more ready to believe an entrepreneur's or a star fund manager's vast fortunes are down to their intellect and acumen. Whilst Fortuna demanded passivity and resignation to her ways, fortune now favours the bold, the astute and industrious. Fortune has been secularized, democratized and is at the command of an individualistic capitalist economy. Fortunes are actively *made*. And the business world applauds those who do the making, while sparing little thought for those who stumble on the ascent. There are few business books about losers. Their fortunes don't interest us.

Shakespeare stages the eclipse of the earlier concept of Fortune by the new. Timon's fortunes are due entirely to his lack of judgement, his prodigality, his inability to manage resources, and his obstinate disregard of prudent advice. The play is more like a parable of bad business than a classic tragedy. Indeed, while most of Shakespeare's tragedies are identified as such in their full titles (some even with promotional puffs, such as *The Most Excellent and Lamentable Tragedy of Romeo and Julie'*), the play's full title is merely *The Life of Timon of Athens*. That's life, we shrug.

Timon learnt his lesson in the school of hard knocks. Too late came the recognition that money makes the world go round. But this is not news to us. So what can modern, hard-nosed business—that doesn't believe in Fortune, but does in making fortunes—learn from Shakespeare's parable? Perhaps the lesson for business is to reverse the understanding gained in the unfolding of the play. This is not to naively prescribe Timon's former philanthropy as the way forward, or the renouncement of the golden idol that now turns the globe. Dickens already did that with Scrooge. But, if nothing else, the play restores an awareness of the earlier meaning of Fortune. Perhaps affording a recognition that Fortuna may not have been entirely banished from a world in which we put our faith today.

In a recent book on the subject of happiness, the economist Richard Layard discusses the "Hedonic Treadmill." This is not a new piece of gym equipment, although if a new piece of gym equipment is what you think will make you happy then maybe it is. It is a metaphor used by psychologists to explain why happiness doesn't rise in line with economic growth and material acquisition. As he puts it:

> *living standards are to some extent like alcohol or drugs. Once you have a certain new experience, you need to keep on having more if you want to sustain your happiness. You are in fact on a kind of treadmill, where you have to keep running in order that your happiness stand still.*[2]

---

2 Richard Layard (2006) *Happiness: Lessons From the New Science.* London: Penguin, 48.

This treadmill is the basis of our consumer society. The new wheel of fortune we willingly turn in pursuit of those glittering prizes that carry the perpetual promise of greater happiness. Desire turns the wheel, the wheel drives the markets, and Fortune (500 or 1000) is still honoured. Both micro and macro economics declare that more is always more, and the only way is up. Eyes forever trained on the upward curve, there is less readiness to acknowledge, as the Poet puts it, "the foot above the head" (FTSE above the head?), or the wheel beneath the graph. Advertisements for investment vehicles are compelled to carry an FSA warning that past performance is not necessarily an indication of future performance, and that shares can go down as well as up. Despite being managed by these new masters of their own fortunes, shit still happens. Two speeds has Shakespeare's play Timon up, Timon down. And two speeds have the world's economies. The uncomfortable truth acknowledged in the small print is periodically writ large in the headlines of the financial media. And so the wheel that provides the emblem for Shakespeare's strangest tragedy still turns.

A Man of Fire-New Words

Roger Horberry on *King Lear*

Principal Actor: Samuel Crosse

No, they cannot touch me for coining, I am the King himself.

King Lear (Act 4, Scene 6, 83–84)

Say what you like about Shakespeare, he did enjoy his neologizing. The opening quotation, spoken by the newly mad Lear as he rages on the heath, sums up Shakespeare's attitude to the invention of new words. He coined them with confidence and consummate skill. In fact Shakespeare contributed more words and phrases to our language than any other author. Despite the fact some have fallen into disuse over the centuries, Shakespeare's contribution to our word-hoard is an achievement unequalled in the history of English.

Like any self-respecting genius, Shakespeare didn't play by the rules; instead he went his own sweet way with wit and imagination. He changed nouns to verbs (*film*, *champion*), verbs to nouns (*dawn*, *scuffle*), verbs to adjectives (*hush*) and adjectives to nouns (*accused*). He added prefixes and suffixes (*eventful*, *remorseless*) and subtracted parts of words to form new ones (*impede* from *impediment*). He gave new meanings to old words (*housekeeper* was originally the landlord of a theatre) and compounded existing words to create new ones (*birthplace*, *eyeball*, *cold-blooded*, *softhearted*).

In short, he played fast and loose with every convention of language and won hands down.

Why am I telling you this? Simple: we're still at it. Language is constantly evolving, although the pace of change is far from even. In Shakespeare's day English was undergoing seismic shifts, just as it is today. This parallel is significant. What's more, we coin words for exactly the same reason Shakespeare did—to express ourselves with more accuracy, truth and economy. Despite 400 years of cultural evolution, some things haven't changed.

No one can agree on an exact number, but it seems Shakespeare invented or popularized somewhere between 1500 and 2000 words still in regular use. I make the distinction because it's notoriously hard to be certain where and when a particular word was invented. Neologisms typically arise out of speech and are rarely documented until well after the event. Take *scuffle*, *stealthy* or *successful*—did Shakespeare invent these words to meet a particular dramatic need, or were they contemporary words that somehow missed being recorded elsewhere and were then wrongly attributed to the big man? Both explanations are possible (it isn't hard to imagine such nominally Shakespearean words as *foppish*, *fortune-teller* or *gentlefolk* originating in the streets of late sixteenth-century Southwark) but many of Shakespeare's neologisms are without doubt genuine.

So how did Shakespeare's new words find their way into English? David Crystal, author of *The Cambridge Encyclopaedia of the English Language*, is surely right when he imagines the Globe's groundlings seizing on the neologisms they'd just heard and hurling them at each other on their way home through London's teeming streets, letting the new words live or die on the basis of their appeal and utility. Modern neologisms get the same reception and must pass the same test. We instinctively notice a new word and applaud or sneer depending on all sorts of subjective factors. Those that pass muster take root in our minds, ready to grow and seek out new contexts and usage.

Let's turn our attention to the linguistic landscape into which Shakespeare's new words were thrust. The period from 1500 to 1700 was a time of extraordinary cultural upheaval driven both by the ascendancy of English as the language of learning and the power of printing to distribute new ideas. In the wake of the Renaissance many classical words were added to the vernacular, not that the process always went smoothly. There was much hand wringing and argument concerning their adoption and usage—the so-called "Inkhorn Debate." This once white-hot controversy focused on the use of Latin loan words that struck some observers as unnecessary or pretentious.

Shakespeare was well aware of this struggle for the soul of English and enthusiastically put some stick about on the side of the pro-Latin lobby. Between 1500 and 1659 as many as 30,000 new words were added to English from classical sources and it seems Shakespeare cooked up at least 600 neologisms from Latin ingredients—*dislocate*, *horrid* and *vast* are all examples. He was, like Don Armado in *Love's Labour's Lost*, "a man of fire-new words."

King Lear contributed *blanket* (in the sense of covering), *dislocate*, *divest* (as in deprive or undress), and the verb *to elbow*. *Epileptic*, *flawed* and *immediacy* all made their debut in *King Lear*, as did *noiseless* (a typical Shakespearean suffix word), *radiance* and *numb*. Interesting though these examples are, the real strength of *King Lear*'s language lies in its exploration of speech and power, truth and lies, sycophancy and straight talk, and it's these areas I want to explore next.

The power of words to betray is made clear in *King Lear*'s opening act. Goneril and Regan show they're willing to say whatever's necessary to get their share of dad's kingdom. Goneril claims to love raggedy old Lear "more than eye sight," "A love that makes breath poor and speech unable, Beyond all manner of so much I love you". Regan's just as bad—she declares, "I am alone felicitate in your dear highness' love". Cordelia can't (or won't) play this game. She tries to tell it straight but misjudges Lear's appetite for flattery. In a moment of hardheaded realism out of keeping with her general prissiness, she reflects on the deceptive power of her sisters' language, describing it as, "that glib and oily art to speak and purpose not". Her inability to butter up the old man ends in her banishment, the last act of power Lear manages before his fall. In fact Lear's authority is directly linked to, and reflected in, his language. The key to the whole banishment episode is Lear's power to say what's what. While king, his word is law. Look at his description of Cordelia after he's disinherited her:

> *Unfriended, new adopted to our hate, Dowered with our curse, and strangered with our oath.*
>
> *(Act 1, Scene 1, 202–203)*

Not much room for reconciliation there, then. At this moment, and for the last time, Lear is able to set the agenda through his use of language. Over the course of the play, his words lose their power to shape events or even describe things accurately. When he ends up cursing Goneril and Regan for their cruelty he sounds like exactly what he is—an old man falling to bits before our eyes:

No, you unnatural hags
I will have such revenges on you both
That all the world shall—I will do such things
What they are, yet I know not; but they shall be
The terrors of the earth.

(Act 2, Scene 4, 276–280)

You can just see him—eyes bulging and incoherent with rage. Having lost his power to rule, he loses his power to speak. Perhaps for Lear they come to the same thing.

Events soon go from bad to worse. As his madness intensifies, Lear turns on almost everyone around him:

They are not men o' their words.
They told me I was everything; 'tis a lie.

(Act 4, Scene 5, 101–102)

It's this ability of language to do harm and to deceive that drives *King Lear*. In the final speech of the play, Edgar reacts against the flattery, deceit and lies that have poisoned so much of the preceding language when he declares that we must:

Speak what we feel, not what we ought to say.

(Act 5, Scene 3, 323)

Wise words indeed. But building on Edgar's appeal, what exactly *do* we feel? How should we say it? Modern life is so complex that perhaps the regularly accepted limits of language just won't do. Perhaps we need new words—words that are economical, powerful and efficient.

And that's exactly what we're getting. According to one estimate, by the time you read this English will have gained its one-millionth word. That's a controversial statistic, with much argument surrounding the status (or even existence) of many of these new words. Yet whatever the exact number, I believe the web has invigorated the practice of coinage in a way not seen since Shakespearean times. Thanks to the immediacy of electronic communications we're witnessing a new golden age of neologism, a fantastic outpouring of words and phrases to describe new ideas or reshape old ones. Today, a new word doesn't need to rely on the inherent limitations of literature or face-to-face usage to gain acceptance. If it works, the internet gives a new word an instant global audience.

This process is essential to the ongoing health of our language, yet today's neologisms, particularly those associated with business, are routinely belittled as buzzwords (itself a neologism from the late 1960s and defined as "a neologism gone fad"—ouch). I think this blanket condemnation is too harsh. Many of today's buzzwords—with all their directness, honesty and strangely compelling appeal—are created for the same reasons Shakespeare coined his new words. Despite the intervening centuries, the same solution answers the same need.

Not that this stops the naysayers. They love a good moan. Many well-meaning but misguided attempts have been made to nail our language by prohibiting the introduction of new words, no matter how useful or effective. In the eighteenth century Alexander Pope went as far as petitioning Queen Anne on the matter. In the nineteenth century Noah Webster produced his eponymous dictionary with the explicit aim of fixing and defining US English once and for all. Over a century earlier Samuel Johnson started out wanting to set the limits of the English language with his dictionary, but to his credit ended up realizing it was neither possible nor desirable.

We can go further. Many buzzwords answer a pressing need to capture, distil or reflect a contemporary feeling. They just do it with more economy and impact than the background language out of which they arise—that's why they succeed. Take the neologism *outsourcing*. You may wince, but there is no simple alternative way of describing the acquisition of goods or services from a source outside an organization. No one wants to write out a lengthy description every time they refer to the phenomenon of outsourcing, hence the need for the neologism. One hearing is enough for a listener to instinctively get it. They may groan, but they understand.

Rather than rail against new additions to language why not take the opposite view and see them for what they are—creative additions that allow us to speak with more accuracy, colour and economy? Consider the word "effort" converted into a verb, as in, "Let's effort that right away." Very Shakespearian. The noun "whiteboard" can be similarly transformed—"let's start by whiteboarding our strategy." Then there's the graceful "glidepath," as in "this merger will put our business on the glidepath to profitability." Insidious corporate-speak or hyper-explanatory neologisms? You decide.

My point is that new words are good. Shakespeare understood this, as does anyone who's ever heard a choice new word and surreptitiously slipped it into his or her personal word stock. The evolution of language is as vital—in every sense—today as it was in Shakespeare's time. Successful neologisms are successful precisely because they answer Edgar's plea to "say what we feel." We can't do without them.

Top Banana

Lu Hersey on *Henry V*

Principal Actor: Alexander Cooke

"Frankly, I'm amazed he's kept it together."

"Me too. Wonder what his father would have made of the dreadlocks?"

"Not to mention the nose-ring."

Hal could hear his marketing team—which consisted of Garry and Brian—talking about him as he walked down the neon-lit corridor. He'd only recently become the owner and director of Ice Kool, following his father's fatal heart attack.

"Still, he's not a total waste of space. He's hot on branding. I notice he's got the new logo tattooed on his arm."

"Brian, I think the tattoo came first. Isn't that where he got the idea?"

Hal reached the plant-filled atrium in the company reception area. Brian and Garry's conversation stopped abruptly. They oozed enthusiasm.

"Hal, great to see you."

"Tell us when you've time for a little chat, Hal. Garry and I have been trying to drive some new marketing solutions forward. We've come up with a very—er—cool plan."

Brian, still only 35, had the look of someone whose suit had been welded on at birth. No matter how hard he tried, words like "cool" got strangled in his throat.

"I'm always interested in ideas, dude," said Hal. "What's going down?"

"Let's have a diary-led discussion, rather than opting for the response equation," said Brian. "When are we all free?"

It took Hal a few moments to work out that Brian simply wanted to arrange a meeting. He'd noticed Brian and Garry seemed to find it difficult to talk about anything outside meetings. They arranged a mutually agreeable time slot later that morning when the committee room was free.

"We're really fired up about the new deliverables, Hal," said Garry a few hours later, once the doors were safely closed. "We've been looking at your new product ideas—they're hot, really hot!"

"Or perhaps we should say 'really cool'?" sniggered Brian, delighted he'd managed to say "cool" twice in one morning.

"At the end of the day," continued Garry, "we've done some blue sky thinking with finance and production and we reckon it's Go Banana!"

Hal looked at him blankly.

"You know, at the Nicest Ices Fair in Bournemouth next month.

We're thinking of focusing a serious bid for the Top Banana award."

"Guaranteed space in the freezers," said Brian, rubbing his hands together.

"Profits through the roof."

"Top Banana? You're kidding, right?" interrupted Hal. "What about Phatt & Beardy's? Those guys win hands down every year—you don't seriously think we can compete with them?"

The others agreed it was a challenge. Phatt & Beardy's were currently undisputed champions of the "real ingredients" type of ice cream. But if Ice Kool won, every major supermarket in Britain would have to stock its product. Result.

"I bet your father would have given it a go," said Brian. It was a clever move.

"Then put it there, dude!" said Hal, raising his hand for a high five.

Brian raised his hand uncertainly. He obviously had no idea what to do with it. Then in a flash of inspiration cried, "You're the daddy!" and slapped Hal on the back. Communication with these guys was an ongoing problem.

A week passed by. Rumours about contestants for the Top Banana award don't take long to circulate. Hal hardly had time to run the idea past his old surfer mates, now employed as his New Product Tasters, before the package arrived. Beautifully wrapped and tied up with a big red bow, it was stamped PERSONAL and addressed to him. It took two men to carry it to his office, and practically everyone in the company found an excuse to drop in while he unwrapped it.

"A snowball?" said Hal when he finally got through all the packaging and opened the freezer box. "From Phatt & Beardy's!" He opened the card inside and read:

LIKE YOUR CHANCE IN HELL OF WINNING, DUDE.

"We need to scale some mission-critical solutions, fast!" said Brian. No one had a clue what he was talking about, but it sounded like fighting talk.

"Damn right!' cried Hal, "This means war. And we're going to win."

Preparations began. It was already mid-February and the Nicest Ices Fair was scheduled for the end of March. Every ice cream manufacturer in the land was preparing their new season products and getting ready to jostle for prime space in the supermarket freezers. Hal's marketing team at Ice Kool were getting increasingly paranoid about industrial espionage.

"If Phatt & Beardy's find out our new season flavours, it could seriously disintermediate our best-of-breed initiatives," Gary told him. Hal understood this meant it would bugger their chances of winning Top Banana.

"And we need to action our hero product. Which ball do we pick up and run with?" It was time for Hal to pick Ice Kool's entry for the competition.

While Brian and Garry thought up ways of marketing without actually giving out clues about the product, Hal sought out Ozzy and Spike, his New Product Tasters. They were ensconced in a cosy office off the factory floor, looking out on the goods yard.

The three young men had spent a lot of time together before Hal's father died. After years of experimentation, they had discovered exactly what grabbed the taste buds of a half-crazed stoner at midnight with a bad attack of the munchies. Interestingly, the same weird flavour combinations seemed to have universal appeal. Brian went so far as describing them as "compelling benchmark action-items."

By mid-morning, they'd narrowed the Top Banana entry choice down to three. Playing Gooseberry was a sharp, fruity ice cream made with real gooseberries, Greek-style yogurt and pieces of honeycomb. Global Warming was a subtle blend of fresh lime and ginger cheesecake. Last but not least, Chocolate Genocide was a mix of Belgian chocolate truffle, raspberry coulis and marshmallow.

Ozzy took another big mouthful of Chocolate Genocide.

"The marshmallow sticks to the roof of your mouth," he mumbled, chewing steadily. "Might make you panic."

"Only if you were completely trolleyed," said Spike.

"The thing is, the public—especially women—love anything with chocolate in it," said Hal.

"I read in the International Journal of Contemporary Ice Creams about a double-blind experiment which found only 78 per cent of women could tell the difference between sex and chocolate. And of those 93.6 per cent said they preferred the chocolate."

"Surely not?" said Ozzy.

They spent a few minutes discussing whether the judging panel was more likely to be women or men. In the end they decided everyone liked chocolate, even men, whereas the other two ice creams were the sort of flavours you either liked or you didn't. The entry had to be Chocolate Genocide.

It was then Ozzy dropped the bombshell.

"We sent a pack to Phatt & Beardy's already," he said. "So now they know what they're up against."

There was a moment of shocked silence. Hal couldn't believe his ears.

"You did WHAT?" he shouted. "What the fuck did you do that for?"

"It was after they sent the snowball and you said it was war," said Spike cautiously. "We thought it would be funny to threaten them with Chocolate Genocide."

"Funny? FUNNY? You sent our best product to Phatt & Beardy's just before the Nicest Ices Fair because you thought it was funny?" Hal could hardly contain his anger.

"They wrote back to say thanks for the road kill. I guess it does look a bit Animal Hospital with that raspberry coulis." He laughed, not realizing the extent of Hal's anger.

Hal stomped toward the door.

"You're both fired. As from right now." He didn't even bother to look back at them as he walked out onto the factory floor.

The next day Hal held an emergency meeting with Brian and Garry in his office upstairs. He told them exactly what had happened.

"I don't want them back on the premises under any circumstances," he said, glancing through the window to check the goods yard below. "Why they did something so stupid, God knows."

Brian and Garry exchanged worried glances.

"I'm at a zero base of understanding too," said Brian. "But on the plus equation, we know Phatt & Beardy's called it 'road kill.' We'll just have to drive forward with an alternative, and positive solution."

The men discussed the options at length. Eventually they decided that they'd have to go with Playing Gooseberry and hype the local produce angle. Fortunately the Greek-style yogurt was made in the country.

"With rich, creamy milk from Guernsey cows," said Hal.

"Is it really?" asked Garry. " I never knew that."

"I've no idea, but it will be from now on," said Hal.

"This will really impact on the packaging," said Brian. "We need to recontextualize a more sexy platform."

For the next few weeks, Hal noticed Brian was in his element, with every space in his diary crammed wall-to-wall with meetings. The new, "local produce" angle packaging had to be rushed through, ingredients had to be sourced, and then the shop floor had to go into overdrive to get Playing Gooseberry ready in time.

But by the Wednesday before the Fair, the excitement and momentum had started to dissipate. His employees were completely exhausted, and an air of gloom hung over the premises. Hal noticed that people went quiet immediately whenever he entered a room. He almost wished he hadn't fired Spike and Ozzy. There wasn't anyone else he could ask what people were saying about him.

A sneaky check on his employees' emails after hours helped him get the picture. Apocryphal "road kill" tales had permeated the company. Most of his staff thought it was going to be business suicide competing for the prestigious

Top Banana award against a massively successful international firm like Phatt & Beardy's. Some had even started worrying about their long-term futures. It was time to take action.

On the Friday morning before they set off on the minibus, Hal arranged an emergency staff meeting. At 9.30 AM, 20 employees—his entire sales and marketing team and a few food technicians thrown in for good measure—were sitting round the conference table in the committee room.

The hubbub of conversation died down when Hal came in and pulled out a chair at the head of the table. Gone were the matted dreadlocks, and a diamond stud replaced the nose-ring. Of course he wasn't wearing a suit, but his new "smart-casual" look was obviously very designer and expensive. Murmurs of approval rippled through the room.

"Colleagues," began Hal, emulating Brian in an attempt to reach his audience, "it's time to line up our ducks and make sure we're all singing from the same hymn sheet. Now is the moment to repurpose our action-items. Our survival as a company depends on us delivering our products to the supermarkets of Britain—and driving them on to the world market."

He worried briefly that his team might think he was appealing for more van drivers, but they all seemed to be following his thread.

"I want each and every one of you to take ownership of your essential role in this campaign. Believe in Chocolate Genocide, and your passion will carry to the buyers and decision makers. Believe in Playing Gooseberry and we shall be Top Banana!"

After a further five minutes of hammering home how essential they all were to the weekend campaign, Hal played his trump card.

"To incentivize you all to go that extra mile, I'd like to take this opportunity to unveil my bonus scheme. This is the figure I'm offering to each and every one of you if we win."

Hal flipped the wall chart behind him and stood up. An excited buzz of conversation started immediately—£2000 was written large in fluorescent green marker pen. It was more than enough to unite his team.

"Come on colleagues, let's hear it for Hal, Ice Kool and our hero product!" said Brian.

Everyone cheered enthusiastically, and followed Brian's lead into a chorus of "Who's the daddy? Hal's the daddy!"

It was time to head off into battle.

In the vast, bland expanse of the trade hall, the Ice Kool stand looked impressive. Hal had themed it so the company's Maori-style logo was incorporated into the canopy, printed on the backing boards and on the sweatshirts he'd given out to his employees. His team's enthusiasm was infectious, and they'd taken several orders from the smaller supermarkets before the competition even started.

Particularly popular was the repackaged Chocolate Genocide. Brian had persuaded Hal to rename it Chocolate Ecstasy, and was busy spending his time enthusing to supermarket buyers about the innovative taste customization deliverables—the packet of chocolate sauce included in each carton.

The judging of the Top Banana entries started on Saturday morning. There were 23 contenders for the award, and the three judges all had to sample every entry to narrow it down to the top five. This took half the day. Hal was delighted when Ice Kool got through, though naturally so did Phatt & Beardy's.

In the afternoon the judges resampled the top entries, which involved a lot of spitting in buckets and heated debate. Hal got as close as he could while they were trying Brain Food, Phatt & Beardy's entry. The blueberry-based ice cream seemed to be filled with some kind of pink, brain-shaped confectionery. Clever. And just the kind of thing a smaller company like Ice Kool couldn't risk producing without advance orders.

There followed a long break while the judges conferred. Finally representatives from the top five companies were asked to go the main stage. Although Hal had seen them around at the fair, Phatt and Beardy didn't go up to the stage themselves. They sent the head of their PR company, Alexandra Cook, recently nominated Business Communicator of the Year. Hal wondered if he should have sent Brian or Garry up instead of going himself.

By the time the judges came to announce second place, Hal had bitten off all his nails and felt like he couldn't breathe properly. A few agonizing seconds later he was put out of his misery. Phatt & Beardy's was called up to accept the Silver Banana. He caught Brian's eye. Did that mean they'd actually won? Alexandra Cook made a very short, simple acceptance speech on behalf of Phatt & Beardy's and everyone clapped.

"So finally we come to this year's Top Banana," said the compere. "Based on their excellent idea to promote the use of local produce, the winner is Ice Kool with Playing Gooseberry."

The hall was filled with the sound of clapping and cheering as Hal walked across the stage. Taking the big, brassy Top Banana trophy from the compere with one hand, he leant toward the microphone.

Suddenly the speech he'd prepared about driving proactive deliverables and embracing cross-media cultures went completely out of his mind. "Thanks," he said simply. "I hope my father would have been proud of us."

To his surprise, the crowd cheered and clapped even louder, almost as if they preferred a short speech. As he came off the stage, Alexandra Cook smiled and handed him a business card. Hal smiled back, looked at the card and put it in his wallet.

He glanced over to where Brian and Garry were sitting. It came to him suddenly that his marketing department was due for an overhaul.

Out of This Wood Do Not Desire to Go: Exploring Magical Spaces

Alastair Creamer on *A Midsummer Night's Dream*

Principal Actor: Samuel Gilburne

Night and silence.—Who is here?

Puck (Act 2, Scene 2)

Lying in my tent, it's so pitch dark I can't tell whether it's midnight or time to get up. But I'm now wide awake and gradually register what woke me. Owls are calling across our camp. It sounds as if they're moving, spiralling, and for a moment I'm transported out of this wood. Then someone's cell phone alarm goes off. It's time to get up.

Prologue

To show our simple skill,
That is the true beginning of our end.

Quince (Prologue)

I keep returning to woods—Athenian and Sussex. When reading *A Midsummer Night's Dream* I was fascinated by what took place there. It led me to think about the qualities of certain spaces—let's call them magical spaces—where unusual and unexpected things could happen, where people and relationships could be transformed and transported, where the order of things collapsed and changed, where the unknown reigned, and surprise and possibility lurked.

So I wanted to explore what makes a magical space and to pass on those discoveries to others via this book and associated website, to bring magical spaces into the realm of the possible, within the reach of everyone and their everyday.

I started with a belief that most corporate spaces are far from magical. Special rooms created for a magical purpose—for staff to dream, imagine, invent or simply refresh themselves—tend to disintegrate through familiarity or cynicism. Entropy sets in. The flipchart reasserts its need to exist. Dreams fly away. Chairs and tables come back to roost.

I knew it would be richer to involve others in the journey. That's how eight of us ended up in the Sussex woods for two days, talking, sharing and discovering truths about magical spaces in a magical space. And that's how I ended up in a tent, staring into the morning darkness, listening to two owls, wondering where the hell I was.

This green plot shall be our stage

Quince (Act 3, Scene 1)

Comparisons with the Mechanicals are entirely justified but completely unplanned. We were rehearsing our ideas in a wood, getting spooked by things in the dark, trying to be creative, occasionally brave and ultimately working toward a self-imposed yet unnecessarily crazy task. Because, on the evening of the second day, we were due to present our ideas to a small group of friends on stage at Shakespeare's Globe Theatre. I had booked a two-hour slot as a way of grounding our endeavours.

This is the story of our time in Arcadia.

Et in Arcadia Ego

Occasionally, very occasionally, I get an unstoppable desire to read a certain book. Just before beginning this project something nagged me to re-read *Brideshead Revisited.* I bought an old copy, one with the beautiful cover by Peter Bentley, and breathed it in:

> *"I have been here before," I said; I had been there before; first with Sebastian more than twenty years ago on a cloudless day in June, when the ditches were creamy with meadowsweet and the air heavy with all the scents of summer; it was a day of peculiar splendour…*

I was taking the group to Ben Law's place deep in the Sussex woods. I had been there before; first with some colleagues more than five months ago on a cloudless day in May. It had seemed like Eden then and I knew that if I wanted to do some work around the idea of magical spaces then I should work in a space that had "peculiar splendour." The wood also linked it directly into the play.

I knew that what we had to learn would somehow be enhanced here. What I hadn't anticipated was that a lot of our learning would come directly from Ben and the wood. It is a place of such gifts.

Prickly Nut Wood: our arrival

> *Are we all met?*
>
> *Bottom (Act 3, Scene 1)*

We arrived at staggered intervals with stories of traffic hold-ups, rain and other delays. One of our company never made it out of his M25 tailback. It was only after having heroically assembled a small village of five tents, working our way round trees and foxholes, that we realized we all now knew each other.

I had made no formal introductions and, as we sat down to start, I sensed I didn't need to explain why I had asked each person to come along. We were clear on what we were doing and pitching the tents had made the group one. So why do we always introduce ourselves at the start of a meeting? Some of the time it's appropriate, but once in a while that slight anonymity creates a lack of hierarchy and judgement. And out of that comes the possibility of sharing ideas.

Ben then took us on a walk around the woods. He is a quiet, modest man who is incredibly clear about his values and the way he chooses to live in harmony with his surroundings. He drew us into his world, and his deep knowledge of the woods unlocked a barrage of questions. We slowly climbed up through coppiced sweet chestnuts. Acorns crunched underfoot.

> *that all their elves for fear*
> *Creep into acorn cups and hide them there.*
>
> *Puck (Act 2, Scene 1)*

We collected chestnuts and picked shitake mushrooms. He pointed out the promise of a badger sett if we were to be at a certain spot at dusk. Ben talked about the trees as if he were a godparent—arm's length care but always with the bigger picture in mind. His attention to the cycle of growth ensured maximum regeneration with a minimum of intervention. We were spellbound.

Our walk ended at a stunning oak tree standing in its own space. It felt as if we had been in his presence all afternoon. Somehow he had transported us out of time, like a meditation. In many ways Ben is an artist. As Hockney says, "What an artist is trying to do for people is bring them closer to something, because of course art is about sharing."

By this time we were joined by a new member, Ben's 10-year-old son, Rowan. He came on the walk and knew a lot about the wood. He was a Puck-like figure on the fringe of our group. Later in the afternoon he came and sat on a ledge above our meeting space—just as Puck watched the Mechanicals rehearse their play.

> *I'll be an auditor;*
> *An actor too perhaps, if I see cause.*
>
> *Puck (Act 3, Scene 1)*

That afternoon and evening we talked of Ben and his stewardship of the wood. There was not one iota of ego in how he talked about it—the wood was so much bigger than him. He was not just concerned about the next task or season or cycle. His vision contained decisions that needed to be taken by someone in 100 or 150 years time. This was a wood for generations to come and some of those future guardians might be members of his family whom he would never meet—Rowan's children's children's children.

My time here is the rustle of a leaf

Ben Law

Ben's approach to stewardship meant he was able to stand back and embrace the space, holding the wood in his arms in order to carry it forward.

So we discussed this and applied his example to magical spaces within organizations. We felt stewardship, as a concept, contained three aspects: the intention; the attention given to something; and the letting go of control. When we spoke about magical spaces that had been created by one of us or that we had known, we realized that they lacked this central idea of stewardship—the intention or purpose that led to a vision; the attention that must be paid to the detail of the space and its ongoing relevance; and the creation of space and room for things to happen. You cannot tightly control the outcome or outputs of magical spaces. There must always be the element of surprise, of the unknown.

In that aspect, organizations (particularly corporates) would instinctively resist magical spaces because they can't be fitted into compartments. You can't really predict their value or success, you can't measure them and therefore replicate them with any degree of certainty.

Prickly Nut Wood: evening

Sometime a horse I'll be, sometime a hound,
A hog, a headless bear, sometime a fire;

Puck (Act 3, Scene 1)

Around dusk we huddled round the low fire in the outdoor kitchen. On the grate were two large blackened kettles that needed a coal-stoker's glove to pick them up. Making tea was a conscious act. Not for us the flick of a switch or the ease of pouring onto a perfectly placed work surface. It became a minor celebration, a ritual. After a while, and at no signal, some of us fed the fire, others chopped wood, someone else prepared the wood-burning stove.

A breeze would occasionally swirl the smoke into one of our faces. If it got too bad we stood up and found another seat in the square, eyes moist. A couple of us preferred to stand, anticipating the smoke and moving round the group.

The fire became the heart of our conversation. We needed it for heat but more importantly it framed how we spoke to each other. On one hand it made our conversation dynamic because we were all moving in relation to something we couldn't control. On the other, and I don't know how it did this, it made us listen.

Prickly Nut Wood: morning

I have had a most rare vision. I have had a dream,
Bottom (Act 2, Scene 2)

We drew our thoughts together mid-morning when minds were turning to the Globe Theatre presentation that evening. It became clear that we had collectively circled around the same ideas, through our experience, the conversations we'd had and with our contact with Ben. We knew what we wanted to say, we just didn't know how to bring our experience of the last 24 hours to life on stage for our guests. And that's when we got pulled back to the oak tree.

Yesterday, Ben had introduced it to us, the oldest tree in the wood, at least 350 years old, and a place that he visits to think and reflect. He showed us an old lightning scar and other places where the tree had healed itself. Could this tree be over 400 years old, I asked? Possibly, he said. We realized that this tree might be as old as *A Midsummer Night's Dream*, written between 1594 and 1596, more than 410 years ago.

At this time of year, the scattered acorns were sprouting and beginning to send roots into the ground. We had our connecting idea. We collected several cupfuls with the aim of giving everyone an acorn from Shakespeare's Oak (now newly named). Shehani took a photo of the tree and a copy of that would be offered as well.

We agreed that we would start by asking our guests whether they thought the Globe Theatre was a magical space. Then we wanted to introduce the ideas of stewardship, being between the worlds, invitation, dedication and ritual, talismans and finally connection. We quickly assigned roles, who would say what, packed up our stuff, thanked Ben profusely and drove up to London.

Interlude: driving from the woods to London

meet presently at the palace; every man
look o'er his part; for the short and the long is,
our play is preferred ...
No more words. Away! Go, away!

Bottom (Act 4, Scene 2)

On stage at Shakespeare's Globe Theatre

Gentles, perchance you wonder at this show;
But wonder on, till truth make all things plain.

Quince (Prologue)

At 5.30 PM we were led into an almost empty Globe and gathered in the courtyard where the groundlings stood. A breeze swirled around the theatre. The last tour party of the day shuffled out from an upper balcony. Silence. I took a deep breath and started:

If we offend, it is with our good will.
That you should think, we come not to offend,
But with good will.

Quince (Prologue)

I asked if people thought the Globe was a magical space. The first answer was no, it was what happened here that made it magical. Someone else talked about their memories of great evenings past that made it magical whenever they were here.

During these exchanges I remember catching the smell of the campfire from my jumper (none of us had changed from the woods—we hadn't had time). I heard a sea gull cry and for a brief moment I forgot where I was—at sea? On board a ship in the hold? It was a moment of complete transportation.

Each of us led a section. Our guests asked questions, made notes, sought clarification. But most of all they listened.

Nick read the closing lines of the play:

If we shadows have offended
Think but this, and all is mended:

That you have but slumb'red here,
While these visions did appear.

Puck (Act 5, Scene 1)

Without planning it, we led the group in perfect symmetry from the courtyard, on to the stage, into the retiring room, back on to the stage and finally finishing in the courtyard. We dedicated our discoveries from the woods by opening a bottle of Silver Birch wine, from the winery close to Ben.

We offered everyone an acorn from Shakespeare's Oak and a photo of the tree from where it came. Over the last two days we'd had a number of connections with mnemonics, talismans and triggers, and this final act of handling an acorn (along with the sea gull earlier) reminded me of how powerful seemingly tiny objects could be and their role in magical spaces in conjuring up other worlds.

Either I mistake your shape and making quite,
Or else you are that shrewd and knavish sprite
Called Samuel Gilburne.

Fairy (Act 2, Scene 1)

There was another presence there that evening that I didn't fully understand at the time. Just as Rowan had been Puck to our Mechanicals in the woods so here in the Globe, Samuel Gilburne made his appearance.

Of course, this is an act of imagination, even fantasy, but Sam, as Puck, assumed a number of disguises during the evening. As a sea gull he completely transported me to the sea. As a wind he made us wrap our coats about us. As a thought he reminded me of the wine I should give everyone at the end. As an usher he told us we couldn't drink on stage which meant we had to end in the courtyard, and that created our symmetry. As an idea he led us to a Greek restaurant (where else) afterwards, where we celebrated our triumph.

There will be days and days and days like this.

Plenty *by David Hare*

Postscript

'tis almost fairy time

Theseus (Act 5, Scene 1)

In preparing for the woods I remember having two conversations with Max and Frankie. Max is five and has a "thinking spot" at home and at school. He talks about both spaces very seriously and showed me what he does when he's thinking. These spaces have a special significance because of how they've been prepared for him. Simple intention, rituals and dedications keep them alive and powerful.

Frankie needs a book to go to sleep. But, being four, he doesn't yet read. What he wants is a book to hold, to tuck under his arm. This can't be any book. It must be one he's chosen. I imagine his body osmotically absorbing the story, his physical connection to the book creating an unfettered flow of pictures and words.

I've been to Arcadia now. It's called *A Midsummer Night's Dream*, Prickly Nut Wood, Shakespeare's Globe Theatre. It's called magical spaces. Even after a long sweet bath, several showers and fresh clothes, two days later I could still just smell the campfire in my skin. However, my notepaper is made of sterner stuff. A week on, the smell is as powerful as ever, the wood-smoke insinuating itself into a distant cousin—like a bloodline.

For a space to become magical it has to have the capacity to allow people, individually and collectively, to change their consciousness, to step into that place between reality and spirituality. If I had to sum it up in a line I'd say that a magical space is where each person can expand their experience of themselves.

> *Between the experience of living a normal life at this moment on the planet and the public narratives being offered to give a sense of that life, the empty space, the gap, is enormous.*
>
> *John Berger*

Consider me expanded.

O Alastair, thou art changed!

Snout (Act 3, Scene 1)

Acknowledgements
My thanks go to the seven wonderful people who accompanied me on this voyage. They are: Ollie Lloyd, Julie Batty, Nick Murchie, Ali Pretty, Romy Shovelton, Shehani Fernando and Amy Clarkson. The following also enabled our journey to happen and made it as rich as it was, so many thanks to Martin Clarkson, John Simmons, Shakespeare's Globe Theatre and, of course, Ben Law. Finally, thanks to Jane for suggesting the idea of the woods in the first place.

If you want to read about how you can create magical spaces and understand more fully the concepts and ideas we discovered and how you can apply them to your own spaces, please go to the 26 website (www.26.org.uk) where you will find a link through to magical spaces.

The Confessions and Confusions of a Clown at the Court of King Corporate

Fraser Southey on *As You Like It*

Principal Actor: Robert Armin

Enter Fraser Southey, a writer of moderate talent

What's the first thing you think of when someone says "Shakespeare" in polite conversation? With me, it's usually the Chandos portrait. The one where he looks like some moon-faced roadie from the Midlands, complete with old-rocker earring and zany moustache/goatee combo. Or it's *that* Hamlet line—the most self-absorbed obsessive rumination in the history of light entertainment: "To be or not to be blah blah blah ..."

Wrong play of course (this being a self-absorbed obsessive rumination about *As You Like It*); and to my way of thinking, also the wrong line of enquiry. I mean, I can't speak for any other writers in business, but I don't spend much time up on the ramparts, wondering: "Whether 'tis nobler in the mind to suffer the slings and arrows of outrageous fortune, or to take arms against a sea of troubles, and by opposing end them."

For me the big, cold-sweat-inducing dilemmas revolve

around whether I've got too much or too little work; and whether "'tis nobler" to work for a climate-changing oil major than a child-choking cigarette manufacturer.

So forget Outrageous Fortune vs Sea of Troubles. Can Shakespeare make me a literary genius? And how do I get to be that famous? Those are the questions that interest me. What follows is an account of my efforts to find the answers and (being a writer) share them with the world in blindingly brilliant fashion.

Enter William Shakespeare, a playwright of prodigious talent, and Robert Armin, a Shakespearean clown

If you want to know how famous someone is, you Google them. If you want to know how much more famous they are than you are, you Google yourself and divide their total by yours. I Google "William Shakespeare" (21.9 million links), "Robert Armin" (3.89 million links) and "Fraser Southey" (4 links); 21.9 million divided by 4 gives me 5,485,000,000, which means Shakespeare is 5.5 million times more famous than me. The same equation tells me Robert Armin (an actor pal of Shakespeare's and one of the original cast members of *As You Like it*) is 0.97 million times more famous than me. Still, it's good to know where you stand in any relationship—particularly threesomes, which can be difficult.

Enter Charles Lamb carrying a small package from Amazon

I open a new Word document: "Shakespeare Thing". I write a promising first line: "There are two of us in this story. One of us is famous. One of us was famous. The other is a complete nonentity." Then I order two books from Amazon: the Penguin Shakespeare *As You Like It* and the Penguin Popular Classics *Lamb's Tales from Shakespeare*. I crib the plot from Lamb then tackle the play: in easy-to-swallow chunks over several days, usually while lying on an orange recliner in my back garden. It isn't bad. In fact, it's pretty good, although the plot falls to pieces at the end of the second act. So, probably not vintage Shakespeare, I decide.

"Good but not great," I write in my Shakespeare Thing Word document. Reassuringly like most of the corporate guff I churn out.

Enter a bald Swede

Then something comes up. Called the World Cup. For 30 days I do nothing except watch football, discuss football, read about football and write down football results on my *Times* World Cup Wall Planner. I forget *As You Like It*, I forget Shakespeare. Reopening my Shakespeare Thing Word document on Monday 13 July, I decide my promising first line is actually crap. Just like England in fact.

Enter three brothers, two dukes, two cousins, one wrestler and my daughter

I find Esther (aged 10) reading the Penguin edition over breakfast. "Men have died from time to time … chomp … and worms have eaten them … chomp … but not for love—ugh!" She fake-gags, then asks me: "How's your Shakespeare Thing going Dad?" I tell her straight. "Not good." She fires straight back: "Use up words telling the story. That's how I fill space in my Reading Diary."

So I add a sub-head to my Shakespeare Thing: SYNOPSIS. Then I write: "French court—two brothers bicker—one fights wrestler—girl falls for brother, brother falls for girl—both banished—girl (disguised as boy) flees to forest with cousin and clown—brother and aged retainer follow—brother writes love poems to girl—girl (still disguised as boy) teaches him to 'woo'—brother learns boy is girl—his girl—brother and girl married—ditto many other minor characters—all return to court (except another moody brother)." I word count the document. Good news: I'm up 74 words from 25 to 99, but still some way short of a viable first draft.

Enter a challenging reinterpretation pursued by Ross Kemp

At last. Something clicks ideas-wise. I don't know how or why—but I'm off: the bumper A3 pad on my desk a great steaming mess of insights and telling observations. Out they squirt: one striking similarity between imaginary sixteenth-century French court and twenty-first-century corporation after another. Power shifts, power struggles, power players, power dressers, cross-dressers … Only one doubt dangles. Striking as my similarities undoubtedly are, do they really constitute "Blindingly brilliant?" Aren't they just a teeny-weeny bit "Blindingly-bloody obvious?" *Mea culpa.* I see now why theatrical troupes spend so much time replaying Shakespeare in contemporary settings—Antony (Blair) and Cleopatra, Mac~~beth~~Bush, The Merry Wives of [Charles] Windsor, that kind of stuff—it's just too easy. I'm at it myself; a proper Peter Hall, plotting every detail of my own challenging reinterpretation: the limiting confines of court recreated as Limited Company, rival dukes reborn as rival directors, Rosalind now an oestrogen-charged female exec, Charles the Wrestler (*the* perfect comeback role for Ross Kemp), the sinister head of Corporate Security …

Enter a different state of mind

Only one bit doesn't fit: the Forest of Arden. A problem this, because Arden is where most of the play happens. "Play" being the apposite word, because that's how most of the characters in Arden pass their time. Playing bows and arrows. Playing dressing up and let's pretend. Playing mums and dads. I'm with Celia (the usurping duke's daughter) on Arden: "I like this place, and could willingly waste my time in it," but I can't fit it into my contemporary reinterpretation. Who could? Forests just don't figure very prominently in corporate life. I try Arden as gardening leave, Arden as corporate bonding experience, but neither convinces. Then it hits me. I can't place Arden because Arden isn't a place. It's a state of mind. Something else hits me too, with breathtaking clarity. Forest-wise, I'm missing the wood for the trees. I'm already in Arden.

Flashback to a stressed-out creative director pursued by demons

It's that phrase of Celia's: "waste my time." It sets me thinking about my 20 years (so far) as a writer for business. How

I wasted the first 17 of them in pursuit of wealth, power and creative clout—first as an advertising copywriter, then as a creative director/rent-a-presenter. Until year 16, when I went "Pop." Nothing deadly, no coronary or stroke, just a series of dead-awful panic attacks that warned me in no uncertain terms—clown time is over! I went freelance soon after, into self-imposed exile from the Court of King Corporate, only to a 30-foot patch of weeds in south-east London rather than a forest in France.

Enter another writer bearing gifts

Another stupid mistake. Over lunch I tell a writer/friend I'm doing: "A little something on Shakespeare." Over coffee, he drops a bombshell.

Friend: *"What's your take on the Seven Ages of Man speech?"*
Fraser: *"The seven ages of what?"*
Friend: *"All the world's a stage, and all the men and women merely players ..."*
Fraser: *[Thinks] "Shit! I've missed the most important bit!"*

I check the Penguin edition. The speech isn't there. Pages 40–43 are missing. Bloody Amazon! No, scratch that, they're there—fused together by some kind of yellow crud. Squashed Frosties! Bloody Esther! I tease the pages apart. Only the last of Jacques' famous lines is Frostie-free: "Sans teeth, sans eyes, sans taste, sans everything." To which I might add: "And sans hope."

Enter Alan Rickman as Robert Armin

I have a dream. I'm asleep in bed but I know I'm dreaming because my wife isn't my wife. My wife is Alan Rickman, lying beside me, fully togged (thankfully) as lovable Shakespearean clown Robert Armin. "If all the world's a stage," he booms (projecting horribly), "And all the men and women merely players, WHAT PART DO YOU PLAY IN THE PLAY?"

Enter a great many pleasure-seeking Belgians

"What part do you play in the play?" Rickman/Armin's dream question pursues me, even to a remote gite complex in south-west France. Here, on a family holiday, I fall into company with a crowd of pleasure-seeking Belgians, determined to undermine my Shakespearean labours by urging me to: "Join us for a beer in the pool!" I should heed their advice, instead I make yet another stupid mistake. I read a history book: *1599 A Year in the Life of Shakespeare*; author James Shapiro, an academic who hails *As You Like It* as one of four masterpieces (*Henry V*, *Julius Caesar* and *Hamlet*, the other three) written by Shakespeare in just one year. 'Nowhere else in his works does Shakespeare break the frame in quite so disconcerting a way,' I learn. 'Not only of its time but also ahead of it.' I'm gutted. "Good but not great." it says in my Shakespeare Thing. Good but not great my arse!

Enter a corporate writer playing with his parts

The days and my Shakespeare Thing grow shorter, the deadline for a first draft draws closer, and still that reedy voice in my ear: "What part do you play in the play?" Clearly, drastic action is required, if only to get Rickman/Armin off my back. I decide it's time to follow up my Google fame test with a deep-immersion experiment.

I wear a pair of my wife's winter tights (forest green). Over these, a pair of outsized shorts, held taut against my thighs by elastic bands, then pulled up to create a puffball effect. I wedge my feet into a child's pair of curl-toed Aladdin play slippers, then top the whole ensemble off with a voluminous white shirt, unbuttoned almost to the waist. Feeling suitably Shakespearean, I withdraw to my office to find my part.

Enter the writer as romantic lead

Orlando first. Pulling in my stomach, I declaim to the mirror: 'O, Rosalind! These trees shall be my books, and in their barks my thoughts I'll character …' Pausing, momentarily, I pick up a Swiss army knife for effect: 'Run, run, Orlando; carve on every tree the fair, the chaste, the unexpressive she.'

The part feels natural on two counts: one, Orlando is a romantic and so am I; two, Orlando is a crap poet, ditto moi. But on every other level it doesn't work. Orlando is young; I'm middle-aged. Orlando is slender; I'm stout. Orlando is surprisingly strong for his size; I'm surprisingly not for mine.

Enter the writer as proto-Hamlet

I put down the Swiss army knife, pull what I hope is a melancholy expression and tackle Jacques. All seven ages, from "infant, mewling and puking" through to "lean and slippered pantaloon," complete with actions. Emboldened, I repeat the performance for my wife (a voiceover agent), also reading her a description of Jacques from the James Shapiro history: 'He has significant presence in the play (speaking almost a tenth of its lines), but no effect on it. He changes nothing, fails to persuade or reform anyone. Mostly he likes to watch. He's melancholy, brooding, sentimental …' She pats me, not unkindly, on my forest green behind. "A self-obsessed, impotent loudmouth," she says. "Yes, it could be you Fraser."

Enter the writer as clown

A small, tinkling brass bell (all that remains of a long-eaten Lindt chocolate bunny) adds motley authenticity to my Touchstone. "The truest poetry is the most feigning," I trill, sensing almost immediately that I have hit the mother lode; that despite the age difference (approximately 406 years) Touchstone's words still ring true for me—and indeed, for anyone else who ever wrote a dishonest word to earn a crust. Or bitched about clients—"The more pity that fools may not speak wisely what wise men do foolishly." Or railed against unnecessary rewrites—"Since the little wit that fools have was silenced, the little foolery that wise men have makes a great show." Or cursed clients who just don't get it—"When a man's verses cannot be understood, nor a man's good wit seconded with the forward child, understanding, it strikes a man more dead than a great reckoning in a little room."

Go Touchstone! A great reckoning in a little room—tell me about it. A fellow writer for business or I'm a Dane's dead dad. "O sir, we quarrel in print." O sir, we do indeed.

Enter Fraser Southey as Touchstone

At last. I have my part(s). At worst I am Jacques: moody, melancholy, fuelled by impotent rage against the corporate machine. At best, there is just a touch of Touchstone about me; sufficient enough wit to push words in unexpected directions; to help a few people see a very small part of the world in a slightly different way.

I've learned something too. About life in general and about my life as a writer in particular: that people don't change, not even if you give them 400 years (so perhaps a little more patient acceptance of clients' frailties and foibles is in order hereafter); that those with power (but without imagination) will always need those with imagination (but without power), so a good corporate clown is unlikely to be out of work for too long; that life at the Court of King Corporate suits Type-A high achievers better than sensitive B-list copywriters.

Most importantly, I've learned to love my lot (family, sanity, the company of words) rather than lust for what I lack (fame, riches, the company of fast women). To take life "As I find it and as I like it" you might say.

Epilogue

As Rosalind concludes (almost): "It is not the fashion to see the writer the epilogue." Only, to hell with the fashion—and with Shakespeare. After 400 years in the spotlight he can spare me 15 minutes' reflected glory before I slope off to an eternity's obscurity in my back-garden Arden. So I get the last line, and I leave you with this thought: "I probably won't die rich or famous, but I may just live a happy writer for business."

Exuent all.

The Will of Others: And the Battle with Cynicism

Mark Griffiths on *Othello*

Principal Actor: William Ostler

Obsessions. I have lots of obsessions. Some last a few months, some a few years, some a lifetime. I go up and down a lot. Like Othello, it depends on the conversations I have with people.

The invitation to become obsessed with Shakespeare came just after I'd been to see *Othello* in German. I live in Stratford-upon-Avon, just around the corner from Anne Hathaway's house. Ten minutes' walk from the RSC, where they are staging every Shakespeare play before reconstruction works begin to make the two major theatres in Stratford the centre of the Shakespearean world they deserve to be.

This *Othello* was a modern adaptation, with subtitles trying desperately to keep up with a flow of foul language. I couldn't understand everything. But it was all held together by the power of a manic pianist, centre-stage, representing the taut and anguished emotions of Othello.

I empathized with Othello, the outsider. The professional man who, after doing a good job, just wants an easy time with his missus. But also a man given to insecurity and anger. And to obsession. A man apart.

In any walk of life, including modern business, it's very hard not to be in with a crowd, to remain true to yourself.

Since then, I've often regretted having this play to write about. It's so deep, dark and wholly unpleasant, it initially depressed me and my first drafts were as bitter and unwholesome as the play itself. But I'm also glad of it. After thinking and talking about it more, rewriting and rewriting, it has made me question why I'm a writer and understand my battles with writing in the marketplace.

For those not familiar with *Othello*, and for those who don't relish the thought of 200 minutes of heaviest-duty tragedy, here's a quick synopsis which will be useful to us later.

Othello, a Moor from North Africa, is commander of the Venetian forces come to protect Cyprus from invasion by the Turks. He's had a long, successful military career and is newly married to Desdemona, a woman only a third of his age. The drama revolves around Othello's right-hand man, Iago, who hates the Moor and secretly plots against him, embroiling Othello's fearful and unwitting officers, Cassio and Roderigo, and feeding all Othello's insecurities about the differences between him and his young wife. The tragedy resolves when Othello murders Desdemona, then commits suicide, while Iago is caught and brought to justice. In a sense, there is no justice—this is a very dark play and one that leaves a bitter after-taste. Full of insecurities, it makes you wonder what state of mind Shakespeare was in when he wrote it.

Before we discuss how the relevance of *Othello* fully came home to me, let's just put Shakespeare in the picture here. The man was part of a theatrical company for which he wrote, acted and performed administrative duties. As a co-owner, he even financed it. During Queen Elizabeth I's reign, he was part of a company called the Lord Chamberlain's Men. In 1603, when King James became monarch, Shakespeare's company was co-opted to become the King's Men.

History tells us that the period 1603–05 was fraught with political tension, as the country waited to learn the direction in which the new monarch would take it. The foiling of the Gunpowder Plot in 1605 took that direction firmly in favour of the Protestant ruling class that Henry VIII had first established 60 years earlier. As principal writer in the king's company, Shakespeare produced a string of tragedies during the first three years of James's reign—*Othello*, *Timon of Athens*, *King Lear*, *Macbeth*.

People have described these as the heaviest of Shakespeare's plays from a writer who had produced at least 25, including light comedies such as *A Midsummer Night's Dream*, *A Comedy of Errors*, *Love's Labour's Lost* and *Much Ado About Nothing*. Shakespeare's father had died in 1601, the political climate was strained and here was a successful writer with a great responsibility for a whole company of men. Not only had he to write in censorious times dangerous to dramatists, he had to please the new king and continue being successful. The pressures on this writer must have been immense. He must have felt very lonely, isolated, alienated, full of insecurities, as a writer, as a man. Welcome to the world of Othello.

There is a clear transition in the life of Shakespeare, from the earlier period when he was able to combine light comedies with history plays around the documented lives of monarchs, to the later period full of world-weariness and obsessive tyrants. During this transitional period, he wrote what people have come to call his "problem plays"—such as *Troilus and Cressida*, *Measure for Measure* and *All's Well That Ends Well*—which have happy endings but also include elements of tragedy. *Othello* resolved the problem, being the first of what was to be almost his entire future direction, in which he seemed preoccupied about the rise and fall of tyrants.

From this point on, Shakespeare's plays show a battle in which cynicism and bitterness feature powerfully and sometimes successfully. Iago is cynicism personified, the voice inside the writer's head as much as in Othello's ear, that plants negativity and preys upon fears. Only when I came to understand this did I realize why *Othello* is so important in our discussion of the relevance of Shakespeare to modern business.

Oh, and just because *Othello* is so desperately dark and just because it is one of the few plays in which Shakespeare made no gesture toward the light, I'm inserting my own clowns' interlude bit right here in the middle of my script. Shakespeare wrote some heavy-duty stuff and knew when to tell a joke or two. Some of the overly corporate reports we see could do with a little bit of the clowns' interlude.

But what on earth am I talking about? You know, that bit in most Shakespeare plays where there's a song and a dance and a bit of a laugh between two old fools? Usually after two characters with names like Domino and Exfolio return from the wars to find that Exfolio's maiden love, Unliklia, is due to be married to the tyrant of Venice. They attend a masked ball. There's nothing like that in *Othello*, which feels a bit like working your socks off all year only to discover there's no Christmas party—the one time and place where many of us regularly lose the plot, where we can let slip our mask, or swap clothing under the table with our colleagues, forget our everyday professional reputation. Just like Shakespeare, really. Hardly surprising then, when Domino and Exfolio swap roles, as well as clothes, and it may well turn out that Unliklia is Exfolio's long-lost little sister after all and that Exfolio marries Domino, who was a woman dressed as a man all along. It doesn't really matter. Laugh with it. Then, exit, followed by the plot.

Doesn't this mask-wearing and role-swapping tell us a deal about the lot of the modern business writer? About how very difficult it is to be yourself when working with a host of different clients? Never was a writer more mindful of his clients than Shakespeare, yet it seems to me that, whenever he introduced the clowns' interlude, he was putting himself into his writing. Thanks for reminding us of the need to do that, Will!

At times, when it's impossible to don a mask or act a role, a writer simply has to do what he does best. Shakespeare is celebrated for the sheer variety of his output, yet he knew very well how to recycle his best moves and plough the same old furrow year after year. And, like Shakespeare, we may find ourselves saying the same thing for clients but with a different take on it—on a product, on a website, in a brochure, in a DVD, in a book. Same stuff, different smell! That's what successful writers do. They say one thing and they say it over and over again. After all, it's hard standing apart from the crowd. Especially when you're a man of service. Like Othello.

Writing for business is all about service. We writers are doing the will of others. Yes, we have a choice with whom we work and for what we work—for money, for meaning, for whatever. We work in a business culture. *Othello* tells us about this business culture in which we have to operate and become effective. Nothing's changed much. In 1606, countries fought over turf. Today, it's companies. And then, within a company, there's all the in-fighting. Greed and envy. Cynicism and self-interest. Cronyism and oneupmanship. Recognize the territory? You've got the map. Poet, would-be-novelist, scriptwriter, this is the world you joined when you became a writer for business and had to earn your living—a world full of characters, all claiming to be writers, all as competitive as hell.

If all the characters in Othello were business writers ...

- **Othello** would be the professional writing consultant brought in to do a job. A man with experience, a specialist, well respected. Damned good at his job. But a loner. Not a man to join in. Despite standing apart, he wins hearts and minds in competitive battles: a true writer; he's retained and rewarded, recognized as the author of the project's success.
- **Iago** would be the failed hack turned in-house communications manager, whose role is to ensure Othello gets what he needs. He wants the comforts of position, yet is consigned to internal newsletters and craves to have his name against the great works that Othello is praised for. He's able to feed thinly disguised destructive ideas to his unknowing readers, who see him as an honest, upstanding, salt-of-the-earth type, even as they succumb to his poisonous drip-feed about Othello. He'd probably have his own blog, but under a pseudonym. He writes on toilet walls, starts corridor conversations and lets others finish them. He stirs things up, while keeping the corporate mask on. Like a sour journo, he uses people for sources of info, takes the credit for himself, then stabs them in the back—literally, in this case.
- **Cassio** would be the writer who's been with the company many years and grown with it. Now he's a loyal brand manager who wants to protect the brand. He controls his weaknesses (drink and women), but is no match for Iago's manipulation—he is wounded physically, but fears he's lost his working reputation.
- **Roderigo** is the junior copywriter. OK at his job, but

never going to set the world alight. Until Iago makes him think he can. Iago edits his work and sends Rod in directions that serve only his downfall.

- **Emelia** would be the personal assistant—not there for her writing, but to support the others in theirs. Experienced, wise. Doesn't trust her boss, but keeps her mouth closed until she senses injustice. She turns whistleblower. Very brave.
- **Desdemona** would not be a writer, but writing itself. Loved by Othello until told she is no good. Then he's ready to destroy it and doubts his own abilities. Iago, Cassio and Rod are all happy to claim it for themselves—but, too late, Othello destroys it. Unlike Othello, we can destroy our first drafts and start again. We have to improve on it, remain true to our passion.

I can't escape the haunting meaning of *Othello*. It brings me constantly to my own personal motivations. What makes a writer? What makes *me* a writer? We're all different. But we have to find our own way to control it, or be controlled by it. Not for nothing does the object of all our joy, our heart, our home—our own passion for writing in the first place—our Desdemona, contain the word "demon" within it.

Othello shows Shakespeare as a man right in the middle of this struggle to control or be controlled by his demon. Here was a man who wanted desperately to write to live rather than live to write. He was his own Othello, a man who had done his duty, performed his tasks and who stood at the top of his profession. Pushing 40, all he wanted was to go home to Stratford and live the quiet life. When you're tired of London … you're tired of London. He was compelled by corporate and political reasons to start his career with King James over again. And the first fruit of that is *Othello*. In a sense, it shows Shakespeare giving in—idealism has lost. However, if so, why not name the play after its central character, Iago? In the title of the play, Shakespeare is showing us the true goal of the writer—to overcome his demons and rediscover his values, over and over again, whatever the provocation, whichever unpleasant vagaries the business culture throws at us. Othello, the fount of all true values, is more important than Iago, the source of the world's ills.

Even so, Othello was a successful general but

Shakespeare portrayed him failing as a man. Even after 25 plays, Shakespeare was looking at himself, addressing that self-doubt all writers have, revealing how a writer must succeed as a man first, or else his legacy is nothing. And Shakespeare kept this struggle at the forefront of his writing from this moment on.

Shakespeare in love, Shakespeare in London? In *Othello*, we've caught Shakespeare in crisis. Othello is Shakespeare's own vulnerability—admitting he was a human being first and a writer second. And this is the struggle I recognize myself facing every day as a writer for business. We are not pure conduits or word machines. We have to stand up and be counted. We do not have to be so in love with a company that we never question it, so that our writing for it becomes bland. But we always have to fight negativity, turn it into something creative and channel anger into a force for good.

We are surrounded by cynicism masquerading as humour. Our brutish Big Brother culture assumes it's cool to slag off everyone and everything, so long as it's done with wit. Values are portrayed as dogma and victory as success. We are driven by our media to ridicule difference and to destroy what works. As we begin any business meeting, the little Iago voices inside our heads wonder about hidden agendas and manipulative messages, adding to the chaos of communication. Our role as writers in this business world is to make sense of this, to avoid being drawn in to the insider gamesmanship, to remain the outsiders—the professionals who are friends with the client but not in bed with them and unable to challenge. How do I reconcile my values with the client's values? This is a question we have to answer every time we pick up a pen.

Ultimately, I volunteered for this task because I found the proposition preposterous. Namely, that Shakespeare had anything to say to us about writing for business today. Now, I know better, because I am reminded that, in spite of it all, we have to stay true to ourselves and not be swayed away from our own beliefs, the reasons we began writing in the first place and what keeps us at it day after day, year after year. Let *Othello* be our lesson when, like Shakespeare, we are doing the will of others. We all have an Iago inside us. What is your Iago saying to you?

Uncovering the Malvolio Within

Katherine Peñaloza on *Twelfth Night*

Principal Actor: Nathan Field

I am Malvolio. But so are you. There's a bit of Malvolio in us all, for deception is endemic in human nature and relationships. Like Malvolio, we are all sick of "self-love," prone to suffer from varying degrees of self-deception as evidenced in the lies that we tell ourselves to feed our vanity and self-esteem. And, like the characters in *Twelfth Night*, we are just as likely to be both victims and perpetrators of deception—to deceive as well as to be deceived, sometimes willingly.

The idea that deception is prevalent in our lives fits easily in the context of modern business. Deception is pervasive because work is by nature competitive. There are people to manage upward and below. Relationships are complex and often fraught with clashing and hidden agendas. Just as companies compete for market share, people are also often pitted against each other in pursuit of the same rewards. This in turn breeds a self-serving climate inclined to dishonesty. But far from taking a cynical view of human nature that would condone criminal acts of deception, *Twelfth Night* simply prods us to look closely at the lies, deceit and dissembling that transpire in our daily life. To question them, to be aware of them, even if we have to accept that they are the stuff of ordinary humanity.

In his depiction of Malvolio, Viola, Orsino and Olivia, and their respective deceptions, Shakespeare makes us consider whether it is not in fact people who wilfully choose to believe in what they would like to believe in. We are all deceivers and self-deceived. Appearances are as misleading as words, and we are continually trying to discern the meaning of other people's words and actions, while obfuscating our own. Olivia and Orsino are just as culpable as Viola for their deception because they cling to their views on love, which colours their perceptions. Words and their meaning are elusive, and we know this from our own attempts to crack the secret code in Shakespeare's texts; deception is commonplace as nothing is ever as it appears. Face value does not exist but only what we read into it. Just as there are an endless number of interpretations of *Twelfth Night*, people will read their own meaning and gravitate toward their own preferences.

The deception and self-deception of Malvolio

Deception takes its most interesting turn in the character of Malvolio. There is close interplay between the ruse concocted by Sir Toby, Maria and their gang to deceive him into thinking that Olivia is in love with him, and the delusion fuelled by his own vanity. One feeds on and amplifies the other—the deception to deceive the self-deceived into deceiving himself further. Far from being the innocent and passive victims of other people's deceptions, we are accountable for what we perceive and choose to believe. Just as we are deceivers, we are also complicit in our own deception.

Malvolio is a character completely deluded in his secret desire "*To be Count Malvolio …*," indulging in flights of fancy to marry Olivia in order to elevate his social position. He imagines "*… Calling my officers about me, in my branched velvet gown, having come from a day-bed, where I have left Olivia sleeping.*" In his private moments, he ponders on the significance behind the most inconsequential words and actions of others, and hungrily distils deeper meaning from them to feed his self-deception. A casual and perhaps even throwaway comment can attain even greater meaning for him.

> *Maria once told me she did affect me; and I have heard herself come thus near, that should she fancy, it should be one of my complexion. Besides, she uses me with a more exalted respect than anyone else that follows her.*

Malvolio's excessive pride and self-love thus provide fertile ground for Sir Toby's deception. His delusions of grandeur make him an almost willing victim for Maria's forged letter. However far-fetched, he eagerly quizzes the letter for clues, distorting its meaning to reaffirm what his heart desires:

> *… M.O.A.I. doth sway my life …*
> *… "I may command where I adore." Why, she may command me. I serve her, she is my lady … And the end: what should that alphabetical position portend? If I could make that resemble something in me …*
> *M … Malvolio! M! Why, that begins my name!*

We read what we want to read. Like Malvolio, we bend the meaning of words until they resemble something we seek.

Words are not what they seem

In the last 20 years, modern business has undergone a quiet revolution of sorts in the workplace. Coinciding with the trend toward downsizing and streamlining, the walls have come tumbling down as companies moved to open-plan offices and trimmed layers from their organization charts, ostensibly to reduce costs but also to encourage greater transparency, communication and productivity among their people. But the stripping down of offices and titles has only caused greater unease and uncertainty among people.

It seems that the Elizabethans discerned status from the colour of a person's clothing. Some of this lingers in the dress codes of modern life. But now we eliminate offices and titles, denying people the established symbols of rank and influence in the office. Where once a corner office served as an accurate proxy of one's position and importance in an organization, we no longer know exactly where we stand in the modern workplace. As a result, we become even more sensitive to the minutiae of office life, reading and imagining more meaning into things than might be warranted. Years ago, the partners in an office where I worked hit upon the idea of hot-desking to optimize the use of limited office space. But this plan failed almost immediately as people jockeyed for position, claiming desks that placed them in proximity to people "on the rise." Invisible spheres of influence demarcated the banks of hot desks, and woe betide the naive or ignorant who occupies a desk in the area mentally designated as Siberia.

The same holds true for the way we communicate. Today, talk is cheap in more ways than one. Millions of emails, texts and instant messages are exchanged remotely every second of the day. By opting for speed and convenience, we have traded away the visual and verbal clues that help us discern the intent and agenda of others, making it more difficult to decipher what is implied from what is said. The throwaway nature of the way we text and email also means that we now read far more into the timing and other details of the communication than the actual message itself. With sentiments reduced to abbreviations, commas and brackets, are we any less deluded than Malvolio, as we struggle to make sense of what is really being said? IYSWIM.[1]

Recently, a director at my company chided me for an e-mail I had sent to everyone announcing several new business wins. Surprised that such an innocuous note could offend, I listened anxiously as he pointed out a number of areas in which my email had been glaringly remiss. In the "cc." list, I had placed a less senior person's name before his. Although most people knew that he was the more senior of the two, he was concerned that it might give the wrong impression, causing others to speculate wildly. I reeled at the likelihood that I might have set off a wave of intrigue with my careless placement of his name. It gets worse. In congratulating the people involved, I had blithely listed their names in no particular order, not even alphabetical. A grave error. Inadvertently, I had deracinated people of their rank. Until then, I didn't realize that people scrutinized and read so much into these things.

I now realize that words can be imprecise because even the most seemingly anodyne can be interpreted in several ways. Their meanings are apt to change according to the intentions they contain. In Viola's exchange with Orsino about the inconstancy of a woman's love, words not only help disguise the truth, but also push secret agendas. To

---

1 If you see what I mean.

Orsino, Viola is an increasingly trusted servant. There is growing closeness in their relationship. But we know that Viola, in her disguise as a man, is really speaking as only a woman can. She knows

> *Too well what love women to men may owe. In faith, they are as true of heart as we ...*

By alluding to her secret love for him, Viola takes advantage of Orsino's trust and plants the seeds of intimacy.

Deceivers and self-deceivers all

Perhaps words continue to elude us simply because we are *all* deceivers and self-deceivers, particularly at work. We know this and we choose to be this way, because the key performance indicators placed on us shape our behaviour, rewarding us when we act our roles well. Viola insists to Olivia: "*I am not what I am.*" We do something similar at work despite exhortations to "*be honest and true to yourself.*" Few if any would openly express the true notion of who they are, what they think and what their real aspirations are, because the conventions of the workplace militate against it and the downsides in doing so are great. Instead, we subsume our other non-work selves. Like Malvolio and Viola, we adopt disguises in the form of a facade or persona that we believe fits our given role and its accompanying expectations better than our true selves.

The same applies to companies and the conduct of their relationships with customers and employees. Upward or 360-degree feedback, for instance, is one of the most deceitful practices in modern business. Companies do it because they want their employees to think that they are concerned employers. Managers go along with it because they'd like to be seen as enlightened individuals open to criticism. Of course, we know that in reality honesty does not always pay, because criticism stings and lingers. But we go along with this annual charade, suppressing our true opinions because we'd like to be regarded as "team players."

Malvolio's undoing is essentially to pretend to be what he is not, in direct opposition to what is expected of him. Initially, his serious if rather priggish demeanour befits the persona of a senior member in the household of a lady of standing. Yet, we soon discover that his gravitas is merely a facade, and a flimsy one at that, to disguise his snobbery and hide his dreams of social elevation. Maria deftly dissects his acting and personality:

> *The devil a puritan that he is, or anything, constantly, but a time-pleaser, an affectioned ass that cons state without book and utters it by great swathes; the best persuaded of himself, so crammed, as he thinks, with excellencies, that it is his grounds of faith that all that look on him love him …*

His downfall comes when he allows his vanity to overcome his better sense, exposing his unbecoming though essentially true nature as an arriviste and thus opening himself up for manipulation.

Malvolio's pride, self-love and, above all, his presumptuousness in wishing to change the social order to benefit himself, is punished harshly in the play. All of us harbour secret aspirations, but obscure these to throw others off the scent of our true desires and intentions. We worry that, if exposed, we may appear overly ambitious and deluded, or our actions and intentions henceforth may be misconstrued as self-serving. There is also something strategic in not letting the competition know that you are also after the same prize as they are.

In contrast to Malvolio, the outcome of Viola's deception is positive and rewarding to the main characters involved. Viola's disguise was initially an expedient one that enabled her to enter Illyrian society and establish herself in the household of a nobleman. It not only brings her close to Orsino, but also enables her to express her thoughts and enter his. But a key difference from Malvolio is that even when disguised, Viola speaks with much clarity, self-knowledge and honesty. Despite the confusion caused by her deception, Viola is rewarded with marriage to Orsino.

And so to work

If work is built on a web of lies, and we are all complicit in the deception that transpires, then what does this say about integrity? Or about the well-worn adage "honesty is the best policy"—particularly, as we see in *Twelfth Night*, when some forms of deception are punished while others are rewarded? Integrity is a word that has been liberally used in corporate mission statements worldwide, yet we have also witnessed in recent years a stream of corporate shenanigans. Has overuse of the word resulted in the loss of its meaning?

If anything, this confirms that words lack absolutes. Imbuing them with a sense of morality is almost as futile as cementing their meaning. Much of what we say at work, including many of the supposed facts that we deal in, is prone to misunderstanding. Despite communicating more today, how often do we truly feel that we say what we mean? If we do, then why do we seem to spend even more time clarifying ourselves and unravelling the misunderstandings caused?

In the 2002 production notes of *Twelfth Night* at the Globe, the actors are made to recite a scene without stopping or pausing at any punctuation marks. The idea in this exercise was to override how the actors usually learned and delivered their lines, forcing them "to doubt their lines" so that they would eventually arrive at a better understanding of the text. Like the Globe actors in *Twelfth Night*, perhaps we also need to unlearn our lines and doubt the words we use in order to come to a better understanding of them. Just as nothing is as it appears in *Twelfth Night*, with words we can only ever hope to come to an approximation. So, when people or companies talk of integrity, rather than taking it at face value, perhaps we should consider it as, at best, a statement of intent. One company's mission statement prided itself on four key values: respect, integrity, communication and excellence. That company was Enron.

Postscript

Nathan Field, listed 17th among the principal actors in Shakespeare's First Folio, was born to a deeply religious family. His Puritan father famously preached against plays as "schooles of as greate wickednesses as can be" and agitated for the closure of London's theatres. Ironically, Field became one of the leading actors of his time, receiving the ultimate compliment from Ben Jonson: "Which is your

Burbadge now ... Your best actor, your Field?" In contrast, Field's elder brother followed family tradition and rose to prominence in the Church, although amidst rumours of corruption and deviousness. Field himself was said to be a heart-throb even as he probably performed many of the female parts at the Globe. Along with fame, he also achieved notoriety by allegedly making the Duchess of Argyll pregnant. Two paths cannot have diverged more greatly, yet each associated with deception. But don't take my word for it.

The Comeback Kid is Now the Corporate King

Andy Milligan on *Henry IV*

Principal Actor: John Underwood

On the eve of AngleLand plc's biggest takeover bid, John Underwood looks back on the career of its young CEO, Harry Bolingbroke V, and argues that his transformation from dissolute playboy to heroic business chief was all part of a carefully thought through plan, one from which other business leaders would do well to learn.

Cast your minds back three years. Harry Bolingbroke has been thrown in jail for an assault on his father's Legal Counsel and police are questioning him about an alleged robbery. It's the darkest scandal of his youth, a youth that has been characterized by numerous reports of drunkenness, womanizing and "dodgy dealing" with low life. The tales of the excessive partying of the self-styled "Prince Hal," heir to the Bolingbroke fortunes, and his cronies, especially the notorious Jack "Fivebellies" Falstaff, who is the national Field Sales Director for Bolingbroke, are legion. They have been openly discussed at boardroom level and are a constant source of anxiety for his father. These latest excesses force his father, Henry Bolingbroke IV, to consider kicking him out of the family business.

Now fast forward six months. Harry has played the crucial role in fighting off a hostile takeover bid from the Percy Group and is being acclaimed as the natural heir to his father's empire. Fast forward further to today, and he stands on the brink of pulling off an audacious bid for Francoterre that would make AngleLand the biggest company of its kind in Europe. How did it all go so right?

Popular myth has it that Harry wasted his youth because his father did not give him anything worthwhile to do. Then, during the Percy crisis, Bolingbroke Senior was forced to give his son a role. Harry rose to the challenge, transforming his father's opinions, and his fortunes. So the story told today is one of luck, timing and redemption. I don't agree with that myth. I was fortunate enough to be with Harry Bolingbroke throughout that whole period and was privy to many of his secret thoughts. I know he had planned for his eventual succession. In fact, his so-called "waywardness" was a mask as carefully constructed as his current takeover bid.

Henry Bolingbroke IV had made many enemies when he took over AngleLand in the bloody boardroom coup that ousted Richard Plantagenet. He faced a dangerous ride, keeping opposing factions who had supported his bid together. It is clear that he did not want to expose his son, Harry, to much of the boardroom in-fighting and felt he should give him some frontline experience. So he made him national sales director, working with John Falstaff, a decision he would soon come to regret.

Falstaff was a lazy, corrupt, incompetent Field Sales Director whose expenses claims were legendary. He took "young Hal" under his wing and exposed him to excess. He clearly hoped to ingratiate himself with the "heir apparent" as he called him. But neither his father nor Falstaff had the measure of Hal. Yes he was bored in a job that did not tax him and, yes, as a young, single man with money and privilege he certainly indulged himself. However, Hal was determined to learn from the experience and use it to shape the strategy he would pursue as a CEO in future.

After one particularly heavy night of drinking, Hal confided in me that strategy. I was struck by its clarity and simplicity, but also by the almost ruthless conviction with which he expressed it. He was, he explained, deliberately creating a bad impression of himself. He wanted to create a popular demand for his reformation which, when it came, would increase his popularity. As he idiosyncratically put it: "I imitate the sun, who doth permit the base contagious clouds to smother up his beauty from the world, that when he please again to be himself, being wanted he may be more wondered at."

That was the main lesson that I learnt from Harry Bolingbroke—you are your own brand manager in business. It is not enough to do well: you have to shape and manage the perceptions of how well you are seen to do, even if that means throwing a few false trails to mislead your enemies, and even if it risks alienating some friends in the short term.

But there are other important lessons that the modern executive can learn from Harry's approach.

Get frontline experience so you can lead from the front

Unlike many senior executives who spend their time cosseted in boardrooms, Harry has always preferred to be out in the field talking with his staff and his customers. This honed his instinct for how to act and react in situations.

The experience of working with Jack Falstaff and his team taught him a lot about life at the sharp end; he learned what people wanted and how they liked to be talked to. It helped him to understand the difference between showing authority, which people want, and assuming authority, which they don't. As Warwick Lord, advising Harry's father, said, Harry "studies his companions like a strange tongue … to gain the language."

He also saw firsthand the chaos and incompetence of his father's organization. Jack Falstaff's deficiencies were grotesquely revealed during the huge sales and recruitment drive Bolingbroke launched to counter the aggressive Percy bid. Badly trained, poorly equipped reps were sent in to the frontline with no coordinated strategy; Falstaff himself dismissed them "as food for canons."

The Percy Group on the other side were disciplined, structured and committed, led by the charismatic Henry Hotspur. Moreover, they were close to outflanking Bolingbroke through a joint venture with the Wales-based Glendower Group. It was Hal, not his father, who saw firsthand the problem, then took over the reins of the campaign. It was the son who re-energized the sales force and, in a spectacularly bold move, challenged Hotspur to a public debate as to who was best placed to run AngleLand. It became a duel that destroyed Percy and made a hero out of Harry.

Think carefully, act boldly

Harry is nothing if not an instinctive leader. He trusts in his judgement and in the judgement of those he trusts. He understands the importance of effective action and especially the importance of the bold act. Whether he was firing Falstaff or taking on Percy, Harry moved decisively. But he is not a "hothead"—he thinks through his actions coolly and carefully. This was the key difference between Harry and Hotspur, who should never have allowed himself to risk the advantage he had in market momentum and organizational competence on such a public duel.

Before deciding to take on the Francoterre bid, Harry commissioned a major legal study to ensure he faced no serious obstacles to his claim. He was not so much interested in what the study would tell him (he already instinctively knew it would favour him)—what he wanted was for others to see a due diligence process had been gone through, that his bid had been properly considered. He had thought carefully about how to act boldly and, thereby, successfully.

Your ability to judge people's abilities will determine your success

The frontline experience he gained gave Harry a great eye for judging people's strengths and weaknesses. It has been, I think, his most important attribute as a manager. It is unlikely that he would have had the same "eye for talent" if he had been working in Head Office all his life. For example, having lived among inveterate gamblers and hotheads, he knew Hotspur's tendency to recklessness and love of the flamboyant would make throwing down the gauntlet of a one-on-one debate irresistible to him.

Having lived among braggarts, self-deceivers and the self-serving, he would know that Pistol (who took over Falstaff's role initially) was a fake and that his father's legal officers, Sly and Shallow, were exactly what their names suggested. Conversely, he had seen the integrity of his father's Legal Counsel, when he had had Harry arrested for assaulting him. Harry was quick to reappoint him to his role when he became CEO, rather than settle a petty score by sacking him. In fact, he publicly praised him for his "bold, just and impartial spirit." But, of course, his ability to judge other people's talents stems from his ruthless honesty about himself. He may have deceived Falstaff and his sales team, he may have misled his father, but Harry never lied to himself.

Empathize with your customers and employees

His skill in judging talent is related to his ability to empathize with people—especially his customers. This essential human skill for the twenty-first-century executive is what ensures that the right customers get the right products in the right way at the right time. It also forms the basis for an effective and motivated organization in which everyone knows their place and what is expected of them. Having seen at close quarters the honesty and courage of ordinary frontline staff, Harry knew how to motivate them during two long and brutal campaigns. He showed that, though he was their leader, he was every bit as human as they were. But empathy is not sympathy. He used his empathy not only to understand how to reward, but also how to punish most effectively—hence the public and humiliating dismissal of Falstaff.

Do what you promise, ruthlessly

There is no place in business for lying, cheating or any form of malicious duplicity. Harry knows that. But business is not a church. Business people need to be honest, but they also need to be ruthless. When they make promises they must be kept. Harry made good on the promise he gave his father after the police investigation. Summoned by his father to explain himself, Harry declared that from then on he would "be more myself."

And he also made good on his promise to Falstaff that he would kick him out the moment he took over as CEO. The threat at the time shocked many of us who heard it; Falstaff himself simply did not believe it, assuming that Hal was joking. I was there and I can tell you he wasn't. The subsequent dismissal of Falstaff and the breaking up of his national sales force was another bold and decisive action. It reassured the markets and the rest of the AngleLand board that their new CEO could be trusted.

Communicate clearly and simply

It is perhaps in the skill of communication that the modern businessman can learn most from this boardroom king. Harry understands the value of talking plainly and simply. Say what you mean and make sure people know what you mean. He has little time for doublespeak, jargon and long-windedness. He becomes highly suspicious of anyone who talks too much or who uses words as a way to obscure meaning. I was minded of this just the other week, during the presentation of the legal report into the viability of AngleLand's claim for Francoterre.

The presentation was wordy, rambling and loaded with jargon, and worse still it was insufferably long. Losing patience and needing a straight answer, Harry interrupted the flow of legalese with the simple question, "May I in right and conscience make this claim?" The answer, though not as succinct, was at least briefer than before, and positive. This plain, direct speech is vital to someone who wants to be known as a man who means what he says. During an altercation in a bar between Harry and Falstaff, Falstaff begged Harry not to banish him from his company when he took over, to which Harry responded curtly, "I do, I will" and, of course, he did.

His gift for speaking plainly meant that he could communicate effectively with everyone. He was comfortable talking with frontline staff and often able to make them laugh (admittedly frequently at the expense of Falstaff—he had a sales team in stitches when he described Falstaff as "fatwitted" and "a ton of man"). But he also knew the language of the boardroom and this enabled him to reassure his father and his father's allies that he would be able to take the business forward. He learnt the "jargon" not so that he could use it, but so that he could understand it and translate it into clear, simple words that others could understand.

One of his key communication skills is his ability to

motivate. On a one-to-one basis or addressing a crowd, he would use wit and intelligence to engage his audience and then set out a clear goal that he knew would be attractive to them, whether he was re-appointing his chief Legal Counsel or rallying his sales force before a major campaign. He would avoid florid metaphors, preferring more direct, yet still imaginative language. His style was in contrast to the windbaggery of the CEO of the Welsh Glendower Group, for example. Where Owen Glendower was all exuberant imagery, speaking of how "the front of heaven was full of fiery shapes" at his birth, Harry used everyday concepts and words—it was clear from the results of the final public duel with Hotspur whose approach was the most effective. Harry's description of the by then failing Percy bid as food "for worms" was one of the most devastating and memorable comments in corporate history.

Harry Bolingbroke's career teaches us all some simple lessons that we should never forget in business: have a noble purpose and a clear game plan (but don't stick to it slavishly), communicate clearly and be ruthless when required in pursuing it.

Above all, remember you are the manager of your own brand. And on that last topic, it is worth noting how important his own branding was to him. When he was a playboy he was known as Prince Hal. Now they call him King Henry V. But he always preferred to be known by what his father called him: Harry. And, regardless of the result of tomorrow's vote at Agincourt, Hal's father—if he were still alive—would be very proud of his son Harry.

Two Guys Walk into a Bar

Nick Asbury on *The Comedy of Errors*

Principal Actor: Nicholas Tooley

There's not a man I meet but doth salute me
As if I were their well-acquainted friend,
And everyone doth call me by my name.
(Antipholus of Syracuse, Act 4, Scene 3)

It's Saturday night and I'm sitting at the bar of the Dirty Duck in Stratford, waiting to meet someone. A neutron walks in and pulls up a stool next to mine. "How much for a beer?" he asks. The barman replies, "For you, no charge." I smile weakly and look back toward the door. The person I'm waiting for is my namesake, Nick Asbury. I first became aware of him a few years ago, when he emailed me out of the blue, but this is the first time our paths will physically have crossed. He's a respected actor and a member of the Royal Shakespeare Company. In fact, I've just been watching him charging around on stage in the Courtyard Theatre, bloodstained and bearded, sword at his side. It should be an interesting night.

The door swings open and a bear walks in. I shuffle along the bar to make room. "Excuse me, barman," says the bear, "I'll have a beer and … some peanuts." The barman says, "Hey, why the big pause?" The bear forces a smile—I imagine he gets this all the time and flash him a knowing look. He goes and sits down grumpily on the other side of the bar. The pub is really filling up now, the post-theatre crowd jostling forward, anxious to get served. One of them has a great big slab of asphalt under his arm. I tut loudly and move aside to make room. "Pint of bitter please," he shouts. "And one for the road."

I'm not entirely sure I'm in the right place. Nick Asbury suggested the Dirty Duck and I know it's definitely supposed to be here, but the sign outside clearly says the Black Swan. I guess it must have changed hands recently. I decide to move away from the bar in search of a quieter spot. Grabbing my drink, I make my way through the crowd, when I practically bump into a guy in a baseball cap and jacket walking the other way. The beard is strangely familiar. "Excuse me ... are you Nick Asbury?" The face breaks into a broad grin. "Yes. Hi Nick—good to meet you." I elbow my way back past the road guy and order a drink for my new companion. Then we head for the garden to escape the mayhem. We eventually find a table and a long night's drinking begins.

Why, but there's many a man hath more hair than wit.
(Antipholus of Syracuse, Act 2, Scene 2)

I start by asking Nick a bit about himself. It turns out he's not only a very accomplished actor, he also choreographs all the fight scenes. No mean feat given some of the swordplay I'd seen earlier. I ask if he has any other talents. "I eat fire," he replies. At this point, I'm already beginning to feel outshone by my new namesake. I decide to steer the conversation toward music, casually mentioning my talent for playing the piano—not exactly to a virtuoso level, but enough to hold a tune.

It turns out Nick Asbury is an accomplished pianist. He has played professionally in some of London's finer restaurants. He has even played piano on *The Basil Brush Show*. Apparently, he was great to work with—a true professional. I realize I am losing the battle of the Nick Asburys. The only edge I have becomes apparent when Nick takes off his cap. His hairline may be receding, but I'm a good few inches ahead of him, despite being a couple of years younger. Maybe, somewhere in our distant past, it runs in the family.

I've decided to buy the drinks all evening—it's the least I can do, considering Nick supplied the theatre tickets and is being so generous with his time. I head back to the bar to get another round.

One of these men is genius to the other.
(Duke of Ephesus, Act 5, Scene 1)

I buy drinks for a few of Nick's friends as well. Four glistening pints sit on the bar in front of me and I await a fifth. Looking round, I notice a weird-looking guy at the other end of the bar—it's William Shakespeare. I sidle up to him and ask him about *The Comedy of Errors*.

The way I see it, the play relies on a highly improbable act of naming. Two sets of twins are separated shortly after birth by a shipwreck, each set washed ashore in a different kingdom. By a strange coincidence, both sets are christened with identical names. So you have Antipholus of Syracuse and his servant Dromio, and Antipholus of Ephesus and his servant Dromio. The action of the play begins years after the shipwreck, when one set of twins arrives in the other's kingdom. Naturally, the first set gets mistaken for the second and all kinds of misunderstandings ensue, until the penny finally drops in Act 5 and everyone has a good laugh about it.

Had the identical twins had different names, the misunderstandings would never have arisen. The story would never have happened.

Shakespeare appears to be a bit drunk, but accepts the general thrust of my argument. "But to be fair," he says, "it's not actually *that* unlikely. When the twins are split up, the mother ends up with one set and the father with the other. Now, imagine they've agreed in advance on their first-choice names. At this point, both mother and father are assuming the other twins are dead. So you can see how it might happen." This strikes me as a fair point. "Besides," he says, "Look at you. Two Nick Asburys—one a Shakespearean actor, the other writing a chapter about me. Strikes me as far-fetched. Anyway, let me get these." He nods toward the row of beers and offers the barman a credit card. I notice the name on the card is spelt differently to the signature and raise my eyebrows. The barman shakes his head. "I can't serve you, mate—you're bard."

I don't find this particularly funny, but Shakespeare falls about laughing. Literally falls about—rolling across the floor, doubled up. "You love puns, don't you?" I say. But Shakespeare is too creased up to speak. He crawls away out the front door and into the night. On the other side of the bar, the bear slams down his drink and runs after him.

The barman watches this with a seen-it-all-before

weariness and then asks me for the money. As he hands me my change, he asks if I'd like a tray. "No thanks," I hear myself say, "I've got enough to carry already."

I to the world am like a drop of water
That in the ocean seeks another drop,
Who, falling there to find his fellow forth,
Unseen, inquisitive, confounds himself.
(Antipholus of Syracuse, Act 1, Scene 2)

Back in the garden, I try explaining my line of work to Nick Asbury. "I supply the words for design, branding and advertising projects. It's about coming up with a certain tone of voice that captures a company's personality, and then telling the stories that bring the brand to life. It can be more interesting than it sounds."

Nick tells me that he occasionally does voiceovers for corporate videos. It's a frustrating business, apparently. Your casting agent immediately shoves you in a pigeonhole and you only ever get jobs that match those rigid criteria. So if you need an intelligent-sounding, professional, Hereford accent, then Nick Asbury might be your man. But if you need a gruff, Cockney geezer, then you couldn't possibly have the same actor. Of course, the point is that actors like Nick are playing wildly different characters all the time—intoning sonorously on a Shakespearean battlefield one minute and getting arrested on *The Bill* the next. In the world of corporate voiceovers, this argument apparently holds no water.

I tell Nick there are some parallels with corporate writing. There's always the danger of getting typecast. You become the go-to guy for annual reports. Or the guy who does websites for law firms. Or the one with the clever wordplay. The vast majority of writers can do all of these things and more—again, it's part of the job.

We harrumph knowingly and finish our drinks. It's time to head back to the bar.

And here we wander in illusions.
(Antipholus of Syracuse, Act 4, Scene 3)

As I make my way back inside, I feel I should prepare my next line of conversation with Nick Asbury. I want to offer him a convincing explanation for why I'm here. It doesn't seem enough that we share the same name. I want to explain that, on some level, the coincidence has a deeper meaning for me—a strange kind of appropriateness. The kind of writing I do relies a lot on verbal coincidences—puns, wordplay, alliteration. You name it, they're all tools of my trade—the pun, especially.

Take many of the classic ideas in advertising, branding and design. "Your flexible friend"—a pun that overlaps a physical characteristic of the product with a benefit of using it. "Labour isn't working"—a pun that helped the British Conservative Party back into power. The "byte" in the Apple logo: a verbal pun expressed visually.

Then you have the brands that deliberately turn away puns at the door. Shell's logo carefully sidesteps more negative suggestions of bombshell or eggshell, instead opting for the natural, seaside variety. Other brands aren't so prudent—like the American automotive company that proudly proclaimed its mission to put "people before cars."

I feel this is worth discussing with Nick Asbury. When I first heard about him, I felt as if I'd become part of a human pun. My name, until now, was a sign pointing in one direction. Now it had a double meaning. My professional life is all about playing with language, and now it felt like language was playing with me. I'd come to Stratford as a pilgrimage to the power of the pun.

I ponder all these things as I walk into the bar. The last thing I remember thinking is, "Christ, that hurt."

Hold, sir, for God's sake; now your jest is earnest.
(Dromio of Syracuse, Act 2, Scene 2)

Two petty criminals are trying to break into a building when a policeman catches them. One of them has a gun. The policeman orders him to hand it over. The other one says, "Let him have it." The policeman is killed by a single shot.

This is a true story. I'm pondering it on the morning after, as I wander through the crowds of tourists along the banks of the Avon. I decide to walk past the pub where we were last night, although my head's far too sore to entertain thoughts of a drink. As I approach it, I notice for the first time that the sign outside reads differently depending on the direction you're travelling. From this side, it says "The Dirty Duck." From the other, "The Black Swan." Hence my confusion the night before. This meeting of two people with one name had taken place in one pub with two names.

I consider this irony as I gaze toward the front door of the pub. It's all coming back to me now. I remember stumbling out through the bar at about one in the morning. The barman had told us it was time to hit the road and the man with the asphalt had taken offence. I remember Nick Asbury and I saying our farewells just there in the doorway, beneath the sign. Nick wished me luck and I said I'd need it. And then we went our separate ways.

I decide I might just manage a drink after all. Making my way to the bar, I'm about to get served when the door opens and in walk a polar bear, a giraffe and a mongoose. The barman looks at them with a heavy sigh and says, "What is this—some kind of joke?" I decide it's best to leave.

Acknowledgments
Many thanks to Nick Asbury for agreeing to meet up.

Rock Fever

Jack Elliott on *The Tempest*

Principal Actor: William Eccleston

This is rather nice. I'm in the bar of the Inverurie Hotel in Bermuda, looking out over the ocean and enjoying a cold beer after the show. We had the usual trials and tribulations getting the thing on and now at last I have some time to myself. It was the first night and there's a bash at the Princess but no invitation *pour moi*. Pish! I have the barman and the pianist for company should I need it—but having said that they've both got the shakes this evening. The locals call it Rock Fever. It's somewhere between claustrophobia and agoraphobia apparently, because of being on a little dot in the middle of nowhere for months on end. They can't wait to get off and I don't want to go back. My attempt to put things into perspective hasn't gone down too well either. When you've watched the plague carts trundling through your city, I said, you're not worried by the odd twitch. Perhaps I could have phrased it slightly differently but I'm too old to care.

I've spread my Tourist Board map out on the table to get my bearings. There's a helpful little box with signposts that tells me we're seven hours' flying time and 3445 miles from London. In my line of work and at this time of night that's a bloody long way from the heaving taverns of Southwark and Blackfriars and, frankly, I don't miss them. I'll be 421 next Michaelmas so it could be an age thing, but ask any jobbing actor where they'd rather be. This is as good as it gets.

Before this gig I'd virtually disappeared, like most "hired hands" down the centuries. WS was so right when he lamented the "poor player/That struts and frets his hour upon the stage/And then is heard no more." Of course, I was delighted (honoured, actually) to be listed as one of the "Principall Actors" in the First Folio, but according to my slum slug agent, that was then and this is now. He's even suggested I strike the credit from my CV because it makes me "too musty." Like stripping a man of his medals on the parade ground! Then again, if you type "William Eccleston + Shakespearean actor" into any of the search engines, what do you get? The scantiest biog imaginable and then reams and reams on Christopher "I won't be typecast" Eccleston and his poxy *Doctor Who*. One reference to my Kastril in *The Alchemist* and the rest just looks like a load of spear carrying (which it was, to be fair, but whoever wrote it wasn't to know that). I cling to the sage advice of a fellow thesp. Having also Googled himself recently, he said, "William, don't compare yourself to anyone. Mozart never did."

So, tonight I raise my glass to WS, who once again I have to thank, but I also salute all the anonymous strutters and fretters out there. We keep our heads down and we keep working. We may suffer the slings and arrows but we rally once more to our tattered banner: "Have Tights, Will Travel." Far be it from me to pull rank *Christopher* but I've now racked up four hundred years in the business and counting. Stick that in your police box, you miserable big shite!

Oh, how sweet. I see on my map that there's a place nearby called the Ariel Sands Beach Club. I may have a club sandwich there tomorrow. I may take my own Ariel with me if I can prise her out of the pool. The hotelier is, of course, referencing Prospero's airy spirit in *The Tempest*. More to the point (and the reason I'm here and not admiring the view from my bedsit in Paddington), the first scene of the play is based on Jacobean accounts of shipwrecks in these islands. English shipwrecks, of course—hence all these "parishes" on the map with names like Devonshire, Pembroke, Southampton and Warwick. The whole place is a dream of sleepy England with its red postboxes, driving on the left (20 mph maximum) and its "shall I have a cup of tea or paint a picture" little pickles. Yesterday, I witnessed what passes for extravagant behaviour in Bermuda. An old black man was standing on a traffic island, shouting "you're looking good" to all the drivers. Rock Fever, obviously, but I had to bare my teeth at him.

The literary allusion reminds me of a friend who was playing the usurping king, Claudius, in *Hamlet.* On tour in Dublin, he decided one morning to have a dip in the sea and took a bus to the famous men-only beach that Joyce so memorably describes in *Ulysses*. As he was coming out of the water, an old man who happened to be strolling along the strand called out "Good morning, Your Majesty," and doffed his cap. So light and quick; a complete stranger but obviously an Abbey Theatregoer. I have to age up considerably for Prospero so I don't anticipate a similar scene at the Beach Club.

Yes, we're bringing *The Tempest* home as it were and it must surely be a "first." The play may have been performed here before, I give you that—but outside? On its own island? Hawkins Island—I can just see its lights out in the bay. Granted, we're not doing the whole thing, just the first scene—the actual shipwreck. And there are just the two actors—Sophie something-or-other who plays Ariel (it should have been a boy but that's PC casting for you) and myself. They blew the budget on the set and the extraordinary special effects (SFX), but as the American who does the fireworks told me in the boat back this evening, it is "totally fucking awesome." In fact, he said it was "better than Baghdad," modern weaponry having obviously raised the bar somewhat in pyrotechnic circles. He was also very complimentary about my own performance, which, accustomed as I am to the scraps from the table, moved me greatly. But WS is my true judge. He will surely have appreciated my front-foot delivery; the sheer exuberance I bring to the production. Tonight I did indeed suit "the action to the word, the word to the action" and held "the mirror up to nature."

The adaptation is my own work entirely. It's pretty "free" because we have to feature the car, of course.

It's no good being precious about it. I had a conversation about my proposed textual changes with the powers-that-be at the Globe Theatre on the South Bank recently (not an actor among them!) and I soon realized that, artistically, we're moving in completely different directions. If there'd been cars in Elizabethan England, I said, don't you think WS would have worked them in? Here you are in this thatched place, for chrissakes, when everyone else has got proper roofs and central heating and you're preaching to me about the Bard would have done this and the Bard would have done that. What sanctimonious rubbish! I was there. When we weren't "Closed Due To Plague," we were playing next door to open sewers and walking through mud and shit every afternoon just to get to the theatre. And the audience did too, God bless them. Put a few pustules in your fat pay packets, my good fellows, *then* we'll talk "art."

The theatre's foot soldiers have to cut their cloth. One day you're working for the King's Men; the next day you're working for the Ford Motor Company. 'Twas ever thus. I speak as one who's just completed yet another season of medieval banquets at Leeds Castle. But fortune favours the brave: it was during a "corporate" one night that I made the connection.

I'd liberated a bottle of mead and left the revels to have a stiffener and a crafty fag outside. I was skulking behind a pillar when I overheard these two "creatives" talking. Seems that Ford was taking its global dealer network to Bermuda to launch a new car and needed a bit of serious spectacle in between the business conferences: something enchanting that the dealers could bring their wives and partners to. Obviously, there'd be fireworks—they're *de rigueur* for launches, especially car launches, apparently—but poor Simon and Max, they needed a Reveal, a Big Idea. They'd been out to Bermuda for the obligatory recce and found this lovely little island that was just perfect. But what to do? What to do?

Bermuda, I thought. Hello, I thought. Opportunity, my fickle friend, doth call. All richly garbed in Armani. Are these gentlemen perhaps aware of Sylvester Jourdain's pamphlet *Discovery of the Barmudas* (1610); and a letter by William Strachey, known as *True Reportory of the Wrack*, dated 15 July in the same year? WS certainly was and because he was by then a rich man and moving in elevated circles, he had many friends and acquaintances with financial interests in the New Worlde who, moreover, told strange and wonderful stories of the creatures to be found there. A year later we played *The Tempest* on the London stage and for the first time, audiences saw the magician, Prospero; his spirit, Ariel; and the "salvage and deformed slave," Caliban.

If they didn't know the sources, did they at least know

the play? Look kindly on me gentle Shakebag, I implored, as I cleared the gargle box and launched an impressive gob of phlegm into a floral arrangement. And he obviously did because Simon, Max and I now have a sort of Masonic greeting based on my opening gambit that night. "Ill met by moonlight," we cry, accompanied by copious coughing and spitting.

I don't actually speak in the show: it's all pre-recorded and played back through speakers hidden about the island. Of course, a sound studio can't hold a candle to live theatre but needs must and thanks again to yours truly we somehow captured the necessary "atmos." I held an impromptu casting call at the DSS in Lisson Grove, rounded up some fellow travellers with the offer of copious refreshment and in a spirit of consummate professionalism we wrapped the whole of Act 1, Scene 1, within a week. But although it's high-tech, our production does retain a certain symmetry with the past that pleases me. It's the audience. They meet at the Princess for drinks and then they're brought to Hawkins Island by boat—just as our original Globe audiences were ferried over the stinking Thames; just as the characters in the play are brought to Prospero's island. The car dealers, of course, they know something's up but they think it's just going to be a little son et lumière. What they don't know is that William Eccleston has been waiting for this moment all his long life.

We've built this wooden fort thing on a rocky outcrop. When I say "we" I mean the crew built it—I had to stay in the shade on account of my complexion. (Does Prospero have a tan? I'm sorry, Simon, but my text seems to omit that reference and I have already made a significant concession with this fort business. For my first entrance the stage direction clearly states *The Island. Before Prospero's Cell.* Is a cell not a cave or a rudimentary shelter of some sort? Luckily, Max saved the day. He pointed out, quite rightly, that a fort is an altogether more imposing structure for the deposed Duke of Milan, so I relented. You have to be a team player to survive in the theatre.)

So, from my pokey little dressing room, as the evening light faded and the torches were lit, I watched Ford's finest wobbling up the walkway to my fort, smiling their rich smiles. They're under a spell, I thought, just like the characters I've lured to my island. And the island is a metaphor for the world and also, of course, for the theatre with its power to suspend belief and affect miraculous reconciliation. In 1611 there was an added poignancy to the show because our audience were well aware that this was the last play WS would write as sole author. He said as much in the Epilogue, his valedictory address to the theatre. I was recalling the tears shed after the final performance when I glanced heavenward and saw this huge and very angry bank of cloud out to sea. Just then Max popped his head round the door.

"Mr Eccleston," he said, "there's a bloody great storm coming in. We may have to cancel the show tonight." (September, it transpires, is hurricane season in these islands which is why they'd got such a good deal on the accommodation.) "Never, ever use the c-word in my presence," I cried, laying hold of his throat (which probably accounts for my no-show at the party). "I am in full make-up, I am costumed and I am ready. And so is she." Ariel, poor lamb, was quivering in a corner, but then she is straight out of theatre school. On top of all my other responsibilities, I found myself cast in a mentoring role and it was time to set an example. "We have an audience waiting," I said, "and I believe that's our cue."

Outside, our pre-recorded storm was starting and I could hear the cries of my Lisson Grove comrades, the soon-to-be-shipwrecked mariners. I left the chastened Max and mounted the ramparts. As soon as I hit my spot, I felt the warmth of the lights and the centuries rolled away. On a hillside to my right, a huge sail had appeared to represent the ship being driven on to the rocks. In front of me, I could just make out the audience staring up at my windswept robes. And behind the audience, the most remarkable sight—another audience on a huge flotilla of yachts and cabin cruisers moored in the bay. Word had obviously got around and they'd just come for the fireworks but, no matter, they were still bums on seats. My voice came over the speakers and I lip-synched valiantly:

Prospero: *Hast thou, spirit,*
Perform'd to point the tempest that I bade thee?
Ariel: *To every article.*
I boarded the king's ship; now on the beak,

Now in the waist, the deck, in every cabin,
I flame'd amazement

A laser shot from Ariel to the sail, which promptly burst into flames—perfectly stage-managed technology and a jaw-dropping moment for the audience but a mere bauble compared to Mother Nature. Seconds later there was an almighty flash of lightning followed by the inevitable Jove's thunder. Miles out to sea, the most incredible electric storm was raging and that huge bank of cloud had now blocked out the moon above me. I looked up to the heavens and got the shock of my life. On the cloud, there was this huge figure. It must have stretched for miles from top to tail. I raised my left arm to signal the reveal of the car that was lashed to a pontoon in the bay.

Prospero: *Hast thou also brought the new Ford Focus to the island as I bade thee?*
Ariel: *I have, sir. With Zetec engine safely ensconced.*

I knew that spotlights would pick out the car and I heard the rapturous applause but my attention was elsewhere. This person up in the sky, I realized who it was. It was me. A poor player. They'd lit me from below to pick out my craggy features and my image was being projected massively onto the cloud. When I moved my arm, its arm moved too in this great sweep across the heavens. It was I, William Eccleston, conducting this celestial symphony. I resisted the temptation to redirect the audience's attention away from the car. It was a private moment between God, WS and myself.

Back in the bar now and alone, the tears have at last come.

Ulysses: The Interview

Brian Millar on *Troilus and Cressida*

Principal Actor: Joseph Taylor

Scene 1: Ulysses' office

Ulysses

[Talking into his speaker phone]

Two million shares at dollar twenty five
I wish to dump before our quarterly
Results go to the press. Use my Swiss bank.
Tell no one of this stratagem, my friend.

[Line 2 buzzes]

PA

Young Brian Millar from the magazine
Called *Management Today* has come to hear
About the leadership techniques you used
To headhunt Helen out of Trojan hands
And hear some wisdom that he might pass on
To business people of the present day.

Ulysses

Oh, what a yawn. To be the king of spin
One must pay court to journalists and such.
Just let me find my pinstripe toga and
Then send him up. Two coffees please, and milk.

[Enter Brian]

Brian

Hi, Ulysses, thanks so much for your time. Where can I sit? Great! Do you mind if I use a tape recorder? Does that bother you?

Ulysses

Not in the least. I hate it when I am
Misquoted. And so do my legal team.

Brian

OK, we'll check everything carefully. I wondered if I could ask you about Achilles. Obviously your management styles differed considerably. There were rumours of personal tensions. Could you talk a bit about that?

Ulysses

Did you see the movie *Troy*? It was a flop.
Brad Pitt they cast to play Achilles' part.
A stroke of genius, for the boy is great
To look at, but quite dead between the ears.
The Bradster got Achilles to a T.
He had the look of a great CEO,
Worked out, and bought his suits at Gieves & Hawkes.
But analysts are easy to distract
With perfect ties and hair and pecs and teeth.
You see, Achilles failed. And that's the truth,
Because he let the Trojans make the rules.

When Hector sought a duel man-to-man,
Single combat in front of everyone,
I told Achilles that I always say
Only a sucker gets in a fair fight,
But would he listen? No. Muscles for brains.

(In Shakespeare's play there is some suggestion
Achilles subcontracted out the task
To Myrmidons: that is a total lie.
The boy's not smart enough to delegate.)

So out he went and killed poor Hector. So?
Got covers on *Fortune* and *Business Week*.
On Wall Street, stocks in Troy fell like a stone.
People are sheep. They love a CEO
Who seems to do the job and looks the part.
But did the walls come down? I don't think so.
And where was Helen? Her return was in
The mission statement of our business plan.

One meat-head killed another. Well, it made
Something for commentators on the news.
All journalists are scum. Oh—except you.

The lesson here is: understand your goals,
Don't get distracted by some idiot
Who's looking for a fight. Pepsi's a case
Where Coke appeared to beat them in the war
To sell more cola. Pepsi grew with stealth
In other areas like orange juice
And crisps and Gatorade and Quaker Oats.
Coke sell more cola, aye that is still true.
But Pepsi wins hands down on EBITDA.

Investors too, beware the CEO
With Brad Pitt looks and gravitas in spades
They're often little more than masquerades.

Brian

Wow, that's excellent. Can we turn to the subject of your final defeat of Troy? Obviously your strategy was highly original. Can you tell us how it came to you?

Ulysses

The people/sheep thing as I said before
Is key to understanding all I do.
Your company's beliefs are your great strength.
Your enemy's beliefs can make them weak.

Consider railroads in the US West.
They thought their business was in laying track
And plying locomotives back and forth
From prairies over mountains coast to coast.

In actual fact their business was to move
The goods and people expeditiously.

When airlines came along passengers found
A better way to get from A to B.
Today the US railroads are as shades
Of Titans who once roamed the earth until
They met with a most melancholy end.

What has all this got to do with horses?
When people use the phrase "A Trojan Horse"
They tend to mean a deceitful disguise
And nothing more. I must admit
The literalism of the human race
Is tedious to me in the extreme.
The true lesson's more subtle, but that's good.
Otherwise all the idiots would know
And be just a bit harder to outsmart.

A fool will see just what he wants to see.
You build an armoured military truck
Then brand it as a statue and stand back
And watch the punters queue around the block
To kick the tyres and ask for catalogues.

Designing of the horse took quite some time.
We worked to get the ergonomics right,
As well as textures pleasing to the touch,
And racy lines to captivate the eye
And also ample room inside to hold
A squad of SAS troops and their kit.
Which goes to show that often punters will
Buy objects worse than worthless when you get
The design of them just right. Apple knows.
The batteries on iPods used to die.
The hinges on their PowerBooks snapped right off.
The power supplies on G4s were so bad
Thousands of users sued the company.
Yet demand "Wherefore bought you this Apple?"
The Apple user says, "Design, forsooth!"

Today the *Titanic* would be proclaimed
A classic by designers and the press
E'en as it sank. "How good it looks! How brave!

How clean the lines, how rich the wallpaper!"
Your BMWs and Mercedes
Are just the same: reliability
Falls every year yet none ever lament.
Their cars look beautiful on breakdown trucks.

These are the Trojan Horses of your age:
They contain no troops of malicious intent.
Instead they hide a thing far worse, methinks.
That's mediocrity. Yet still they sell,
These rotten oysters in beautiful shells.

Brian

That sounds like a bad state of affairs.

Ulysses

Au contraire. It's an opportunity
To get rich quick. Or richer, in my case.
I'm King of Ithaca as well, you know.
It's really, really hard to make good things.
And people rarely want them. That's the truth.
My company makes useless, pretty stuff.
And we make billions. Don't quote me on that.
I'll sue the molars right out of your face.
Now please excuse me, I have much to do.
Tonight I'm going home to see my wife
But first I must kill all of her suitors.
My PA will take you to the ground floor.
I'm impatient to read your article,
I'm sure it will be great, I'm such a fan.
You're so much better than that Shakespeare chap
Or worse yet Dante who consigned me to
The lowest circle of Hell, I mean *as if*.
My legal team have had some words to say
To both of them, I'm sure you'll be OK.
Goodbye, good luck—oh, and have a nice day.

The Space Between

Lin Sagovsky on *Love's Labour's Lost*

Principal Actor: Robert Benfield

> *Item that no woman shall come within a mile of my court:...*

Four idealistic young men make impossible rules about self-incarceration in an ivory tower. Enter four drop-dead gorgeous women, here on official business and expecting hospitality. So Venus throws down the gauntlet to Mars, as, banned from the castle, the women camp in a field. The duel plays out in this neutral space—a place defined by the tensions between male and female, art and nature, youth and maturity, artifice and honesty.

It's the essence of human experience. In such meeting places, opposites collide and struggle and eventually synthesize in a whole new order. That "space between" is scary: it's the place of chaos, of paradox, of not knowing, of risk, of inventiveness—and of fun. Venturing into it, we encounter the contradictions within ourselves—and if we truly engage with what ensues, like the eight young people in this play, we confront the opportunity to abandon the romance of neat happy endings and start learning how to be a grown-up.

I had something of this in mind recently when I threw a piece of Shakespeare at a client. We had been working on his personal impact (a name I prefer to "presentation skills" because it has nothing to do with death-by-PowerPoint and everything to do with *your* voice, *your* body, *your* ability to tell a story—however dry your material—in a way that no one else can deliver quite like you). Our sessions had covered all the topics I usually use to help any under-confident non-actor rehearse whatever he or she wants to put across, formally or informally: exploring "mindset" (how to apply emotional truth and specific intention) as well as more technical tools: breath, articulation, tone, pace, physicality …

Familiar territory for an actor-turned-management-trainer. Wacky experiences for most straight-laced senior managers.

The delight with David—as I'll call him—however, was partly his endless playfulness: I could throw any exercise at him, and having given it a go (not without initial scepticism at times), he'd look at me like a child that's just learned to ride a bike without stabilizers and say "That's so *right*! How did you *know*? Yes! I get it! I get it!"

At a deeper level, he validated something of which I'm increasingly aware: that the place of private terror is also the place of real self-knowledge; you have to venture into that field of chaos to allow your real song to rise up. David yearned to feel relaxed and confident enough to stand before a hundred-plus people and tell a joke—or just "be funny." He also thought that no one else in the world suffered a phobia like his about public speaking. In truth, he was beginning to acknowledge the call of some inner impulse that dared him to confront his darkest, oldest demons, whatever the cost. I made it clear, as usual in these situations, that I don't have ologies and I'm not a therapist. What *I* do concerns the serious business of having fun.

I'm normally wary of getting too literary with business people, but David was well up for it; the minute he told me that the most unthinkable challenge for him would be to pretend to be an *actor*—you know, actually work for real on a piece from a *play* (he had a way of daring me to dare him to do the unthinkable)—I knew exactly what speech to give him.

And I, forsooth, in love?

It was an instinctive choice—but in retrospect, I know why it suited him so perfectly. At the end of Act 3, Berowne is racked by warring impulses. Furious about what's happened to him, he's terrified of losing face: the very thing he said loudly, in front of the lads and all, that he would never do has sneaked up on him and overwhelmed his little heart.

Cupid's got him. And he's now going to have to adopt every vocal and physical trait of the archetype he most despises: "... love, write, sigh, pray, sue and groan."

But to ignore the call to the unthinkable would be to ignore his real self. And in recognizing that scary truth, and agreeing to venture into whatever chaos it may lead him, Berowne has fun—*is* funny.

And that's David. Someone who for years has wanted to hide away from the world being bookish. But whose life has tapped him on the shoulder and challenged him to run toward the cliff edge with his eyes shut, whooping with terror ... or sheer joy.

There are no neat happy endings to David's story—not yet, anyway. Re-encountering Shakespeare was not a eureka moment after which he kicked over the traces of his highly paid but hateful corporate role to go out into the world, ready to risk everything in order to follow his heart. But through playing with Berowne a little, I watched him embody something akin to the paradoxes of his own experience, allowing Shakespeare to express for him tensions between selves that think they're one thing when, in fact, they're quite another.

And in the process, we laughed a lot.

Neither actors nor artists in general have the monopoly on exploiting such valuable practices. Playfulness like David's is the *sine qua non* of new thinking; it's the letting go of preconceived notions; of the need to control how things should turn out, how people should behave. It's what we do as children to create something from nothing—an experience, a shared story, a way forward. Playfulness can be daunting in a business world that can't relinquish reliance on logic above all else—but it's the key to operating with ease in the open space of the unpredictable.

For Claire Lautier—the Princess in the recent Washington Shakespeare Theater's visiting *Love's Labour's* at Stratford—that "space between" presents a challenge to be met with *openness*. "I was daunted when I first approached the play. And for an actor, that's a powerful place to be—because you haven't decided anything. It's often when you have the best time. If you stay open, you can converge naturally with the text. I wanted to see what would happen."

Willingness to allow space in which things take their own shape is a fundamental quality for an actor, and a key function of the rehearsal room: a space for trying out anything without prejudgement. It's a serious business—and great fun.

Fun is not synonymous with mere frivolity—i.e. pleasant to experience, but lacking real purpose. Without fun, ideas are unlikely to transcend clarity or logic to become inspiring. Fun is also the means by which the place of chaos becomes truly productive, because having fun takes serious commitment.

Actors call this Energy. Intellectual Energy is certainly helpful, and actors do plenty of thinking about text and character. But intellect is only part of the story—it's vital also to energize the text by getting *physical*. You can't rehearse a play by sitting in a boardroom brainstorming for three weeks. You have to get up and *do*—not least, because moving the body liberates the chaotic, instinctive, creative right brain, allowing it to redirect and reinspire the left brain.

The Washington production opened up a whole physical vocabulary for the cast to explore by setting the play in a 1968 hippie ashram. The men became rock stars—Hank Stratton's Berowne strode about in frock coats and floaty tunics, with the kind of leaning gait learned from posing for a wind machine and a crowd of thousands, eking a squealing solo from a crotch-height guitar. Claire Lautier and her maids were '60s chicks in silver catsuits or micro-minis with platform boots, given to exchanging high fives and striking Jean Shrimpton-style poses with thrusting hips.

More used to the costume of earlier periods, Claire found it truly liberating to "let go my corset"—literally and metaphorically. The director wanted her to wear the boots in rehearsal—which she resisted at first in order to discover the tomboy in the Princess, to "move fluidly through all those selves" before allowing her various costumes to inform movement more specifically appropriate to each scene. (Though, as she reminded me, the physical language of the sexual revolution isn't necessarily more expressive than a carefully exposed ankle in a former era—it's just different.)

The actor trusts physical discovery because it triggers

emotional states, which in turn trigger thoughts that explain your words. In that sense, you work backward to marry Shakespeare's text with what the character is *doing* in any given instant: that's how you "make it your own."

I spoke to numerous actors who had played in *Love's Labour's* as well as actor/directors who know their Shakespeare and/or use theatre practices in a business context, to find out what "making it your own" meant to *them*. But for all the interesting, wise and delightful things they told me, I finally realized that the only way I could really get under the skin of that experience in the way I was after was … to play it for myself. So I took the Princess's speech, "A time methinks too short …" to an Actors Centre workshop led by an RSC veteran, Janet Suzman.

I'd performed this speech decades ago at drama school, and having directed it more recently with young auditionees, I know it pretty well—at least in terms of what the words *mean*. But physicalizing it has always seemed something of a conundrum. In every production I've seen, the Princess is static during this speech. Not inappropriately: chaotic encounters played out in the chivalric war zone have been gathering momentum throughout Act 5, as the anticipation of the Russian "visitation" and turning of the joke on the men gives way to the Worthies' amdram and the escalation of animosity between Costard and Armado.

And then Marcade appears. Stop all the clocks. It's grown-up time.

The abrupt change of mood, of season, is Shakespeare's masterstroke—and makes this an elusive moment to get right. The formality, verging on lack of expression, with which various Princesses have seemed to play the ensuing moments is something I've put down to the character's sudden need to appear regal. Self-possessed—on the outside, anyway. But I've never quite felt it fits with what she *says*—and although it may be what the play needs at that moment, to my mind, it threatens to make her cold and dull. The actress Amanda Redman reckoned it's because she's an unlikable prig in any case. In a recent Oxford University student production, Charlotte Cox's performance concurred, seeing her primarily as an intellectual and a diplomat. Claire Lautier's take on that key moment was "All the wild abandon washes away."

They may be right. But in Janet's workshop, all this received wisdom wasn't helping *me*. I made sense of the words all right—but I knew I wasn't truly inhabiting the thoughts, the moments; wasn't making them truly *mine*.

So did Janet. "Did the Princess know she was going to say this or is she making it up as she goes along?" she asked. "She's making it up as she goes along," I said, without thinking. The actor's instinct is all about making a "front-foot choice;" that's the choice that is the most energized, the most interesting—and often the most truthful. And in hearing myself say that, I realized that I just needed to "let go my corset"—to drop all my physical preconceptions and play it exactly like *that*: nothing planned, nothing restricted by assumptions about expected behaviour—neither as the character, nor as an actor. And then the speech took off. Everything your body does when you're coming out with an idea that might be crazy, might be inspired, had to be allowed to happen in my body, and I found myself in touch suddenly with the character's youthfulness and the *lack* of self-knowledge that still wars within her against her capacity for appearing grown-up ("She thinks she's Emily Brontë," said Janet, when I asked her what to make of the self-regard in the lines about "shutting my woeful self up in a mourning-house"). I'd been given permission. So I paced about, at times turning my back on the King, breathing completely differently, energizing each thought ... suddenly I had found the *comedy*, as well as the truth, of a very young and still pretty confused character. A real human being. Someone I could believe in.

Whether those physical choices would work in the context of an overall production is debatable—and irrelevant. The point of the story is that you cannot *know* what physicality will do to your words until you are really prepared to let go of all the head stuff. And no one else can do that *for* you. It's vital to know what the words mean, of course—but if you want to make the message truly your own, you have to get the language into your *body*.

Exploring physicality is the beginning of making a whole new impact—and it has to happen in that "space between." "The body will tell the story" is a mantra I chant to business people who are just beginning to explore the versatility and power of their own non-verbal language. It's no good toeing the corporate line verbally if as you stand there your feet are telling us the wrong story; at some subliminal level, we'll know, and we won't believe in you because we receive the clear signal that you don't believe yourself.

Playing with Shakespeare is only one among myriad ways of giving both right and left brain a space to meet, but he's great for challenging you to commit to the game. (He can even shape your facial expression: David fell about laughing at Berowne's description of Rosaline as his fantasy whore: "a whitely wanton." You can't commit to those words without puckering your lips in imaginary smooching.)

As babies, we put things in our mouths to find out what they are. We play with the physicality of sound in order to discover it for ourselves: to own it and inhabit it. The mouths of business people can be full of words with which the speaker feels no connection. Former RSC voice coach Barbara Houseman describes Shakespeare as "a model of eloquence." Putting Shakespeare in your mouth takes you inside the heartbeat of powerful words. Allowing that heartbeat to drive your whole body takes you on an adventure into fun—where head and heart meet in chaos and the terror of losing control may seem, for a while, overwhelming.

Then, as Berowne begins to grasp by the end of Act 3—and all the lovers stand ready for at the end of the play—you find a new and altogether different Energy, and you know you're starting to emerge on the other side of your confusion into a way of thinking, doing, *being*, that somehow feels far more like *you*.

;-)

Rob Andrews on *Julius Caesar*

Principal Actor: Robert Goughe

Act 1, Scene 2, Line 63

Brutus

Into what dangers would you lead me, Cassius,
That you would have me seek into myself
For that which is not in me?

Cassius

Therefore, good Bru …

Stop!

Hang on.
Whoa.
Stop the show.

Did Brutus just smile there?

He did.

He smiled. (He might even have winked. I don't know, I'm guessing. But it was *that* kind of smile. The sort of smile that might fit nicely with a wink.)

A knowing smile!?

He knows, doesn't he? He knows exactly what's coming, and he's just waiting for it. He's in on it. Wants the fame—the place in history, wants the adulation, wants to be the one being offered the crowns. Him, not best buddy Caesar. He wants it, and wants it bad. He's just waiting for Cassius to whip through some anecdotes and fawning, and get on with telling him that he'd "make a pretty good Caesar too, don't you know," and then he'll snatch the opportunity out of Cassius's hands like a greedy toddler. Oh, line 161 can't come soon enough for wily Brutus.

That is, if I really did see the smile.

(I could be wrong. And if I did just imagine it? Well, then Brutus is an innocent man—Lord Charles to Cassius's Ray Alan. And if he's not careful, he's going to be a silly ass.)

So now I need to check—I need to get the facts straight.

What to do?

Go back to the book, back to the text, back to the line. Quick, quick, before they get to the end of the Lupercal, or I'll never catch them up. There'll be a stage direction I'm sure. Let's look for the bit in italics. "For that which is not in me ... for that which is not in me ... here we go."

What does Bill have to say about this ...?

Nothing.
Not a clue.
Not a sausage.

Where is the high-definition here? Where are the twelve camera angles if you press the red button? I want resolution. I want an emoticon. Quill me an emoticon bard boy. Is it a \;-) or a (:-o ?

I *need* to know.

The whole plays turns here—in the hair's breadth of a gap between the end of Brutus's line, and the start of Cassius's—and Shakespeare has left us to guess. To imagine. To play onto a single line a lifetime of our own dealings, and to make a snap decision about how Brutus deals with Cassius based on how all *our own* Cassi have leaned on us in our Brutine moments, and how we have responded.

Is Brutus a powerful egomaniac desperate for approval? Is he the unwitting patsy to his devious and manipulative brother-in-law, a bit of a sap and a bit of a coward? Both make sense. Choose your conspiracy theory. Play them both out. They are both valid. (Historians can be found to back you up, whichsoever way you go.)

This is more than just Shakespearean shenanigans or "is it a girl, is it a boy?" confusion. This is genuine ambiguity. Carefully constructed, like a hall of mirrors.

In a play that is fundamentally about honesty, there seem to be no right or wrong turnings, and the text alone offers us nothing to suggest which way to go. There *are* no visual clues. There *is* no staging advice, no capitalized shouts or italicized emphasis. All the text offers us is potential.

I have my own favourite play of Italian political duplicity and murder, Dario Fo's *The Accidental Death of an Anarchist*. (Fo, like Shakespeare and the good old days of the *Daily Mirror*, liked to consider the politics of the age and push it back to the masses as enlightening entertainment.) I picked it up at A-level, when we proto-*History Boys* had the time to work our way through a library of theatre history. Clearly, we all found plays that we were never going to see performed. Well, certainly not in Wakefield, where the only theatre seemed to take a season of Duggie Brown in panto for at least nine months of the year. So we read, and imagined. True, reading a play is sort of in the same realm as dancing about architecture, but without the theatre it's all there is and all we had. And reading a play rather than watching it gives one a curious insight. It allows you to see exactly what the playwright wanted you to see, and what he was prepared to leave undefined.

In *Anarchist* like any farce, where comings and goings are so crucial, the description of the stage business is gaudy: A desk littered with papers and files, telephone and a card listing extensions, a bench, chairs, filing cabinet, wastepaper bin, and a coat stand on which hang various coats and hats. He looks like the cliché idea of Freud: wild hair, thin spectacles, goatee beard, shabby suit or mac. He sits calmly. He carries about four plastic carrier bags stuffed with god knows what? (He crosses himself.)

Everything is here. Every last detail. Every prop waiting patiently, every exit covered. I like this—I'm a visual person. My mind's eye is full. I have a very precise plan of the scene. Everything is immutable. Read Arthur Miller—it's the same. Read Tennessee Williams, Neil Simon, Bernard Shaw. Pages of italicized preamble—the size of a broom, the cut of a dress, the spring in a step. Shakespeare's lead-in to *Julius Caesar*, by comparison, looks, well, slapdash:

Rome. A street.

What? Is that it? "Rome? A street?" Is that not a bit vague? Rome is, was, after all, a big place. Are we city centre, or in the 'burbs? Who's going where, and how are they doing it? How many windows are there? How many cobbles? Blimey, you're leaving a lot to the imagination.

And there, dear reader, is the crux of it.

That imagination. That suspension of disbelief.

Anarchist's fourth wall CCTV-picture of a Milanese office is a far bigger deception than the nothingness of a bare floor with a couple of Down Stage pillars and a minstrels' gallery that Shakespeare's Globe has made so familiar to us. Make it a Veronan balcony, a Danish battlement, the Rialto, the Forum. The only thing that the Globe is painted to look like is a theatre, so make it anywhere you want. There's nothing to say it ain't so.

Does the completeness of a modern playwright's vision and the preciseness of their stage direction equal a desire to control? To control the full experience of their theatre, gaffer-taping mark lines to every provincial stage so that this vision is played out in perfect replicated detail? And it is a *vision* too. Read the transcript of *The Rose Tattoo* and you see Tennessee Williams' world in three dimensions—from facial expressions to footfalls to furniture. Read Shakespeare—and it's an awful thing to do, especially if you read the dense, dark, no-nonsense, no-room-for-marginal-notes Alexander Text—and one *sees* nothing. There are no (OK, very few) visual clues beyond *enters* and *exeunts*. It is a game played out in the intellect—a treatise taking the reader from *Oh my God, what shall I do?* to *Oh my God, what have I done?*

But why leave this ambiguity? Ambiguity leads to confusion. We need some decisions to be made. We need direction, don't we? Clarity of vision is a good thing, isn't it?

If *JC*'s text alone offers little guidance as to the meaning of the play—unlike Williams *et al.* who offer it all up on a printer's plate—then it invites evolution and renaissance every time the play is rebuilt with a new cast and a new director. Every interpretation is true, as there is no definitive precedent to say it is false. Split into prerecorded multimedia sound bites for the TV age? In 2003, as it happens.

Gehry-esque cement and post-Communist collapsing statues? Off Broadway around election time, of course. Gay *Julius Caesar*? Well, there are an *awful* lot of men in the cast.

How *do* you build a credible picture, a solid viewpoint from an incorporeal text?

It is, bizarrely, exactly the same question that is posed by those brandingy-corporate-identityish-type people trying to pin down an organization and turn it into a brand. Brands typically don't represent an entire company—there's just too much to represent, just too many possible interpretations—they represent a facet. The facet through which the light is reflected most brightly.

I find the idea of individual interpretative honesty—each one as valid as the one before and the one after—fascinating, but surely it can't be true? The light can't really shine equally in all directions? I am always amused by critics applauding performances full of ambiguity. An ambiguous performance is a dreadful one—it doesn't service the play (or the brand) at all. A definitive performance of a character distinguished by their abstruseness—well, that is something else entirely. *That* is a decision. A conscious act. We make a choice between the possible and the plausible.

I talked to David about it. David is my actor friend. He knows his stuff. I ask him where to start, and when he talks about Shakespeare, he talks about the perils of "disservice." The text is a constant, he opines, it has its poetry and it has its rhythm. Mess with this—the fundament of the play—and it is not just inconsiderate, it is an injustice.

He compares it to singing a song off-key, and he should know. David is in *Billy Elliott*. He's one of the actors who plays Billy's dad. I read a blogged review that said that seeing David was a much darker experience than watching the other dads—he's more drunk, more depressed and more unredeemed by his hoofing kid. But David doesn't do every performance, so even between the Tuesday-night show and the Wednesday matinee, the play is rewritten. I want to know why his *real* is different? Is it part of the process?

"I'm not dogmatic," he says. How so? Well, there is no Strasberg, no Stanislavski, no slavishness to the *Method* in David's method. The Method method dictates that everything can be found within, given the time and conditions to look hard enough. David is more eclectic and all embracing.

He talks about instinct. About investigation. About seeing shards of the character reflected in lots of different places. Every character the amalgamation of a hundred small discoveries—an attitude here, a piece of life history there. Billy's dad's grit is assembled from the blue remembered grit of the Bolton David grew up in. Each of the facets he uses are in their own way not enough to define a rounded figure, but together they make something new and focused.

From that he creates what he believes to be real about a character. Makes an honest decision, one that is right—for him, based on *his* experience and understanding. He has chosen his facet. He has chosen what to be.

We come back to Brutus. He may be only toying with Cassius, eking out a compliment, but he nails *interpretation* brilliantly.

> *...the eye sees not itself*
> *But by reflection, by some other things.*

It's an argument that my design-writer pal Richard and I thrashed out when we were trying to find a metaphor for branding. The purpose of a brand consultant, we proposed, is to be that *other thing*. To be the director, constructing a credible, purposeful and meaningful vision of a company, a product or a plan. And to do so with only the thing that is known to be true—the script (the business plan, the company history, the P&L, the annual report, the marketing plan, all those PowerPoint slides you thought no one would ever see again, all those people who are going to contribute to making it work). Because that's all any organization has, and all there is—and everything else is a deception.

Like David, we find our truth. Make our decision. And then we are steadfast in its interpretation.

(We concluded, in a frenzy of metaphor extension, that branders and theatre directors—so alike in our rimmed tortoiseshell spectacles and black suits (no tie)—even shared the same endgame: to have successfully interpreted the script so that thousands of people could understand it, love it and respond to it, preferably with uncontrolled and excited applause.)

So now, when you look at how a business displays itself, ask yourself the question—how far have they strayed from the fundament of their script? Is that reflection coming back skewed? Maybe, just like in the communal changing rooms in TopShop, they're looking a bit taller, a bit thinner and a bit more buff, and that's OK, so long as the corporate body in the glass isn't a grotesque. We can all accept the truth a touch super-saturated. The things that no brand can tolerate, however, are ambiguity and disservice. Find your truth. Nail your flag to the wall. Don't remain open to interpretation. If your company is about multiplicity, then make it absolutely, openly, joyously, definitively so.

Honesty and self-knowledge are the keys here to success. As any character in a Shakespeare tragedy would attest, if you want to make it through to the end of the play you need to know who you are and to stand up for it. You dither—you die. You lie—you die. You rebrand as "an airline with a global family" at the same time that you outsource all your non-essential jobs ... well, you can see my point.

So, businessmen, take a brander's advice, and remember Brutus, at precisely the point at which he forgot himself:

Into what dangers would you lead me, Cassius,
That you would have me seek into myself
For that which is not in me? /;-)

Acknowledgements

My thanks to David Bardsley and Richard Clayton for their help with this. You can see Richard on DVD in *Les Miserables—The Dream Cast in Concert* and read David's work in *The Sunday Times* and *Design Week*. Or it might be the other way round.

Banished and Englished

Elise Valmorbida on *Richard II*

Principal Actor: Richard Robinson

I saw *Richard II* for the first time in a husk of a building destined for demolition: the defunct Gainsborough Studios. The wide open stage was planted with real grass. It filled the cracked auditorium with the smell of earth and greenness. Real rabbits hopped and picked at it, silent and methodical as stage-hands.

Ralph Fiennes was distinctively, royally Richard, leading a company of other powerful actors. I was moved to tears—not for the themes of death or deposition, the pride that "must have a fall," or the pain caused by traitors and turncoats. My tears were provoked by the play's predominant motif. It's what makes Shakespeare Shakespeare: Englishness.

Richard II is a history of power, but the story is told through the looking glass of Englishness. It is an elegy to the land and the language—an elegy because the tone is reflective and the poet's presence is felt. And because there is poetic mourning in every character's speech: Shakespeare imagining what it must be like to lose his mother country or his mother tongue. Tongues, like tears and blood, are mentioned again and again.

In the effete king's hands, the prospect of losing England is all too real. A humble gardener and a servant worry over the "sea-walled garden" that is "the whole land"—full of metaphoric weeds and pests, unruly growth and strangled beauty. The images are so, so English: fairest flowers, fruit trees, hedges, knots.

John of Gaunt, father of Henry Bolingbroke (the next king), laments:

This land of such dear souls, this dear dear land,
Dear for her reputation through the world,
Is now leas'd out,—I die pronouncing it,—
Like to a tenement or pelting farm

I adore that simple repetition of *dear*, a dear Old English word, so plain and close. It's as if this Englishman cannot get past his attachment. He must keep expressing it, before his national pride must have a fall. He dwells on the dear word, dwells in it. His land is beloved and costly, too precious to lose, but his language is not full of blood-lusting glory or chauvinistic patriotism. His is a happy little well-defended world, majestic in its modesty. It is *Shakespeare's* dear dear land. Memorably, he portrays England's transcendent qualities, repeating *this* like a chant-word for the ephemeral here and now:

This royal throne of kings, this sceptr'd isle
This earth of majesty, this seat of Mars,
This other Eden, demi-paradise,
This fortress built by Nature for herself
Against infection and the hand of war,
This happy breed of men, this little world,
This precious stone set in the silver sea,
Which serves it in the office of a wall,
Or as a moat defensive to a house,
Against the envy of less happier lands,
This blessed plot, this earth, this realm, this England

I too get very emotional about this blessed plot. Maybe my feelings are more extreme because I'm foreign. Every time I return to England from abroad, I gaze fondly at the landscape. The soundtrack in my head is Vaughan Williams' *Fantasia on a Theme by Thomas Tallis*—as lush, as English, as sublime, as Shakespeare's demi-paradise. Yes, dear reader, I am the unofficial spokesperson for the English Tourist Board.

For my real employment, I do words: uncommercial fiction and commercial communications. I teach creative writing. I spent a long time preparing for this work without knowing it. I grew up reading, treasuring, English books. At university I was bewitched by Old and Middle English, the protean Germanic language that appropriated Celtic, and Danish, and Norse, and Church Latin, and Norman, and Flemish, and Dutch ... before accumulating huge, different deposits of Classical Latin and Greek, and French, and Italian, and Spanish, and—

Compared with English, other languages seem so steadfast, so monolingual. Now that I think of it, I wonder if "a Shakespeare" could be possible in any other tongue. He is credited with having the largest vocabulary of any English writer.[1] He imported and innovated more than most, but the language of Elizabethan England was already lush with imports and innovations. And it continued to expand with exploration and empire, acquiring assets from every continent on the planet.

Now I am intrigued by a second language. It's richly international in a different way: English as it is spoken on the other side of the looking glass.

In the country of blinds, the one eyed men are kings.
There is not any ruler without a exception.
It want to beat the iron during it is hot.
With a tongue one go to Roma.
He has fond the knuckle of the business.
Friendship of a child is water into a basket.
After the paunch comes the dance.

These are some of the "idiotisms and proverbs" helpfully listed by Senhor Pedro Carolino in his 1883 *New Guide of the Conversation in Portuguese and English*. His *English As She Is Spoke* is a riotous olde worlde precursor to the current language of trade on the World Wide Web.[2]

1 Albert C. Baugh and Thomas Cable (1978) *A History of the English Language*, 3rd edn, Routledge & Kegan Paul, first published 1951, p. 232.

2 *English As She Is Spoke: or A Jest in Sober Earnest*, first published circa 1880, published by Pryor Publications, 1982, reprinted 1999, pp. 58–60.

Here's a product description written by a specialist about an antique doll for sale on eBay:

Old wrist of porcelain with dickey and back in a same piece.
European porcelain previous to years 20, toy of the baby of the time.
Rare to find it heals it and without breakage nor splits, looking to reflex does not present fissure, crack any breakage.
It does not have wig and either it does not have body.
It presents some dark zones but in his surface, but she is equally beautiful of aspect.
It is of great size since it measures in his height 22 cm (8½") by 20 cm width (7¾")
The shipment will be made once received the payment.

At times this English can be almost Shakespearean. There's a poetic alchemy at work, an unpredictable, transformative verbal play. Transnational transactions take place every day in this bizarre language. It's spoken fluently by automated translation software and by real people.

I have just returned from a European country where the receptionist in a fine hotel asked if my partner and I had consummation at the mini bar. It was not a personal question. In the same trip, we were frequently directed to The Cash—where we could pay—for our anticipated consummation—and a polite notice asked us on every incendiary occasion to collaborate with officials of The Establishment. This is the kind of "material" that sets off any one of Shakespeare's wordsters, from his frothy lovers to his quipping kings to his breathless clowns.

English As She Is Spoke is also the language of some of my creative writing students. It can be hard work sometimes. But, more often than not, it is inspiration for native Englishers: I look to foreign students for the foreignness that brings them fresh to each word and steers them clear of cliché. Samuel Beckett chose to write first in his second language (French) for this very reason. He translated himself into English. It was an antidote to habit. It ensured potency of meaning. What every writer needs to do.

Richard II opens with two dukes fighting. It's Norfolk v.

Hereford, two English territories. Land is identity. Each accuses the other of treason. Each is pierced by "slander's venom'd spear." This is a debate about truth and lies, a battle of words. No, it's a battle *about* words. Words are weapons.

The battle of words is soon ended, not by mortal combat but by a double banishment. King Richard replaces swords with words. Norfolk is banished. And Hereford is banished. The true pain of exile is being shunned from

The language I have learn'd these forty years,
My native English

—Never mind real humans! Banishment for this nobleman does not signify loss of family, or lover, or status. It's worse than losing his life—he's about to lose his tongue.

Banishment from England is no longer the mute punishment it was in Shakespeare's time. English has become the global lingua franca that Esperanto hoped to be. But I can feel the writer's own panic here, as his banished character imagines the horror of losing his verbal identity for ever.

And now my tongue's use is to me no more
Than an unstring'd viol or a harp;
Or like a cunning instrument cas'd up,
Or, being open, put into his hands
That knows no touch to tune the harmony:
With my mouth you have engaol'd my tongue,
Doubly portcullis'd with my teeth and lips;
And dull, unfeeling, barren ignorance
Is made my gaoler to attend on me.
I am too old to fawn upon a nurse,
Too far in years to be a pupil now:
What is thy sentence, then, but speechless death,
Which robs my tongue from breathing native breath?

Lose words and he will lose all of society. That goes for the playwright, the character and the reader—me. Imagine that: being robbed of words. English words. The solitary confinement of aphasia. Imagine that: being robbed of England.

The words *English* and *England* are repeated again and again throughout this play. Here is the first verbal incarnation of "a true born Englishman." He kisses English soil as his nurse and mother, frowns against the French(!), abhors the caterpillars of the commonwealth, sighs his English breath in foreign clouds. Best of all, his word is sterling.

"How long a time lies in one little word!" laments Bolingbroke, hearing that his ten-year exile has just been commuted to six.

Four lagging winters and four wanton springs
End in a word: such is the breath of kings.

Words are everything. They are treasure—"O, to what purpose dost thou hoard thy words?" They are possessions to be transported. They are kinship, of much greater value than noble company. They help Bolingbroke win the throne because he thanks and honours "the common people," rather than talk down to them. (Another Shakespearean lesson in word-power.) Words combine to make the stories that keep dead kings alive: the epitaphs, the legends, the ballads. In other words, words are immortality. For the playwright too.

King Richard asks, "how is't with aged Gaunt?" Shakespeare can't resist a question like that. "Dear, dear" John of Gaunt answers, playing obsessively with his name before he dies:

O, how that name befits my composition!
Old Gaunt, indeed, and gaunt in being old:
Within me grief hath kept a tedious fast;
And who abstains from meat that is not gaunt?
For sleeping England long time have I watch'd;
Watching breeds leanness, leanness is all gaunt:
The pleasures that some fathers feed upon
Is my strict fast,—I mean my children's looks;
And therein fasting, hast thou made me gaunt:
Gaunt am I for the grave, gaunt as a grave,
Whose hollow womb inherits naught but bones.

But then Shakespeare cuts this word-fugue short with the king's weary comment: "Can sick men play so nicely with their names?"

Yet it is Richard who plays endlessly with words, in

comic and tragic ways, to be witty and to impress, as a means of searching out answers to grim philosophical questions. It's as if, by turning words over and over, discovering their hidden nuances and metaphoric possibilities, he can solve the problem of his slipping grip on power. And in a way he does.

Words are power, when all else is lost. The deposed king populates his empty dungeon with verbal subjects:

I have been studying how I may compare
This prison where I live unto the world:
And, for because the world is populous,
And here is not a creature but myself,
I cannot do it;—yet I'll hammer't out.

Yet he'll hammer it out? That's the writer talking, not just the ruler. He's determined to make the metaphor work, despite its doubtful potential. Richard succeeds, perseveres, fills his cell with words. They breed. If it weren't for the assassin who comes to silence him for ever, he would carry on ad infinitum.

And even this final physical deed is rendered verbal. Bolingbroke, now Henry IV, says to the hired killer:[3]

Exton, I thank thee not; for thou hast wrought
A deed of slander, with thy fatal hand,
Upon my head and all this famous land.

The assassin is quick to trace the word back to its source: "From your own mouth, my lord, did I this deed."

And how does Henry respond? He banishes the man—beyond England—to the shade of night.

Do they speak English there?

---

3 As Shakespeare and company "like to play so nicely with their names," I like to think that Richard Robinson, one of the First Folio's Principal Actors, was the man of choice for the lowest and loftiest role in this play of power: royal assassin. A no-name Richard cancels out the big-name Richard. "Grace me no grace, nor uncle me no uncle," says York to Henry. Richard me no Richard.

A World Elsewhere

Gordon Kerr on *Coriolanus*

Principal Actor: John Shancke

A snake of twinkling red and white lights stretched to the horizon. Thousands of pieces of brightly coloured metal were making inexorable progress out of London, under a mid-autumn, pomegranate-tinted sky, car radios spewing out the glib inanities of drive-time DJs or the doleful mutterings of evening news anchormen and women.

Yawning, itching, scratching, stretching, blinking, farting, harrumphing drivers rumpled hair, picked noses, rearranged underwear or snatched glances at copies of the London *Standard* lying open on passenger seats beside them. They smelled their own smells, hummed their own songs, eyes flickering rapidly like the eyes of trapped animals, from road to mirror and back again.

Stopping and starting, the cars moved as one, as if part of the same gigantic organism, each a corpuscle in a giant vein feeding the beating heart of the country's south, countless other identical veins pouring out of the capital from every direction. And from above, helicopters and spotter planes viewed the progress of the various snakes as they crawled away from the capital. They reported back across the airwaves, via aerials and pylons, to tall buildings, their messages being swallowed hungrily by computers and then regurgitated for announcers to read out to the very same drivers who sat beneath the spotter planes and helicopters that were relaying the messages in the first place.

The snake picked up speed and then, suddenly, one driver whose eyes had lingered a little too long on a story about a shooting in London's East End, slammed his foot on the brakes as he almost collided with the rear bumper of the car in front as they all slowed down again. An instant later, as hundreds of feet pressed down hard on metal pedals, one after the other, the road was drowning in a flood of the adrenalin that pumps through the body after such a near-miss. Its bitter taste filled dozens of mouths.

In that moment, chaos theory applied. As when the flap of a butterfly's wings in China can lead to an earthquake in America 24 hours later, so, one driver failed to recognize the faint tingle of a mild heart attack brought on by the surge of adrenalin through his body. Later that night, in a down-at-heel pub in Yateley, he would be buying a lager shandy for his wife, as a prelude to telling her that he was leaving her for a girl from the typing pool, when a second, and much more serious heart attack would lay waste to his body. As he lay on the floor of the pub, a shaft of light from a ceiling spot illuminating his face, like a saint in a painting by Caravaggio, his last words would be: "Sorry … I forgot the salt … and vinegar crisps."

Guy Marks would have smiled sardonically at the ridiculousness of such an episode. People were ridiculous. Life was ridiculous. His contempt for it all was sometimes almost tangible, hanging in the air between him and whatever person he was belittling at the time. His thoughts, however, were otherwise occupied as he nursed his black BMW 750i Sport along the M3 in the direction of his home, 20 miles to the east of where he was now.

They say that the average human being experiences around thirteen thousand separate thoughts a day and at 5.30 PM, as it now was, most of the humans in this line of stalled metal were experiencing something around their nine thousandth thought of this particular day. These sparks of energy darting across the cortex are, more often than not, random—the face of a long-dumped girlfriend, a piece of road driven once in France, that bizarrely anarchic Arcimboldo painting where the head is made up entirely of different pieces of fruit. Random images rolling across the mind like tumbleweed. Not for Guy Marks, though. There was no such thing as "random" for him. Many years ago, one of his teachers had said of him: "He's like a bullet fired from a gun. Only hitting his bloody target will stop him!" Others had said things about him over the years that had been even less generous.

It sometimes puzzled him. He found others so difficult to understand sometimes. Their minds seemed to him like pinball machines. Their thoughts careened off each other and sped off in unexpected directions, setting off other episodes. How could they live like that? But, the sad fact of the matter was that, despicable though others seemed to him, he needed them. They were the key to his progress in the world. Long ago he had learned that to be the case. However, that did not mean that he embraced others with open arms, hail fellow, well met, and so on.

And now here he was, for once a bullet that had missed its target. Not strictly his style, but inevitable, all the same, he figured.

The boardroom was functional. Windows ran the length of one wall, allowing a bored director the opportunity to let his mind freewheel across the office buildings on the other side of the motorway. Glass palaces, gleaming in the sun, empty for the most part.

It had begun so well. He was to make a presentation—his success with this company that had been his life since he had left school followed by his vision for its future. It would be a coronation of sorts. The chairman and directors would have a discussion while he was out of the room and he would then be informed that he had unanimously been voted Managing Director. Or so he had thought.

He had not wanted to go through with this promotion of himself and his achievements. "Do they not know what I have done for this bloody business?" he pleaded with Jim Menenius, the old, sweet-talking, but largely ineffectual Finance Director.

"This is the way it has to be, Guy. Just, for once in your life, be humble and play the bloody game."

And so, here he stood, Menenius's last words to him as they entered the room, ringing in his ears. "Be calm, Guy, please." Playing the game, though, was something Guy rarely did.

It started well. He was not the best presenter, his impatience with the process always showing. He would rather be *doing* than *talking* about doing. It was when his fellow directors launched into a discussion of his management style that the cracks began to show. John Bruton was the ringleader. A sharp-faced and even sharper-suited executive, he directed the operational side of the business and his loathing for Guy had been barely disguised during the time they had worked together. He launched into a scathing attack on Guy's management style. Menenius interrupted, trying to save the day.

"Consider the service Guy has given this company. The hard work, the campaigns, the success of his promotional initiatives."

"Jim, please ..." Guy, embarrassed by Menenius's plaudits, raised a hand to stop him.

"Look," Menenius went on, leaning forward to make his point, "We've all felt the rough edge of Guy's tongue, but we shouldn't take it maliciously. He has nothing but the interests of this business at heart."

At that point Bruton began to list incidents that had taken place over the years, complete with exhaustive detail and each of them highly detrimental to Guy. He ended by saying coldly that he would have no confidence in the appointment of Guy to the senior role in the company. Silence hung in the room like a dark cloth. This was a character assassination that had been long in the planning and Guy realized at that moment he had as much chance of being Managing Director as he had of being Prime Minister. They had all harboured similar thoughts, but had been reluctant to express them.

He looked around the room, disgust on his face, and did the only thing he knew well. He exploded.

"You bunch of pathetic, fucking idiots!" He stared out the window at the road in the distance, cars pulsing onward through the day. "You know I think I even hate the very air you breathe. You have no confidence in me? Well I have no confidence in *you*." His raised voice was by now echoing along the corridors and people working in adjacent offices raised their eyes from computer screens. "How can you turn me down after all I've done for this company? Let's see how you do without me. I hope the competition shows you no mercy. You'll be screwed! Within a year you'll have been taken over and you'll all be out of a bloody job!" His voice lowered to a hiss now. "I'm out of here, this place I have given my all for." He gathered up his papers from the table and began to stuff them into his briefcase. He paused and looked at each of them. "You know something? There's more to life than this." A smile spread slowly across his face. "There is, actually, a world elsewhere."

"You're your own worst enemy!" Menenius spluttered as he breathlessly followed Guy out of the Chairman's office a couple of hours later. "You're lucky to have been given garden leave. If I had been them I would have thrown you to the bloody lions!" They were in Guy's office now and Guy was leaning on the windowsill, staring out at nothing, his whole body clenched with rage. The view from his office had always seemed to him to be like having a corporate hospitality box at the seventh circle of hell. The elevated section of the M4 was even more like a Scalextric track than usual and had never seemed so ludicrous to him. In the foreground, in the waste disposal site underneath the road, stooped, hooded figures sorted rubbish on a conveyor belt, fires raging around them on the wasteland. Every now and then a lorry would arrive laden with the detritus of modern life and dump it into the bin from which snaked the conveyor belt. He looked down on them, a sneer paralysing his features.

"I'm lucky? I'm *lucky*? ..." He turned, squeezing the words between his teeth like rotten toothpaste. His eyes blazed. "*They* were lucky I didn't lay them out one by one! Look at what ..." He slammed his palm on the desk in front of him. "Look at what I've done for this company. I've virtually wiped out the competition. We are so far ahead of them they can barely operate in the same category. Our share price is at an all-time high and I have made each and every one of those pathetic bastards in there rich. I was the one who instigated all the initiatives that wasted our competitors. Me! Not them! They were terrified. 'A little hasty,' they said. 'Don't want to rock the boat,' they whined. And when I did it anyway, they thought I was only doing it for my own benefit: 'If it goes wrong the MD always carries the can; but if it goes right Marks will get the credit.' Not once did they concede that I might, just might, be doing it for the good of the business. Not once!" Again he slammed a fist down on the table, the sound echoing along the deep-carpeted corridor outside.

"Guy, I know all that, but you had a chance in there. All you had to do was play the game a little, get their support, climb down from your high horse instead of galloping into the bloody sunset on it! You needed their support to become MD. And you almost had it."

"Never, Jim." His voice now low and flat. "Bruton and his cronies had it sewn up from the start." He smiled ruefully. "So, I go in there, looking for their *votes*. I present my successes, my achievements to get their *votes*. I lower myself to the level of that … that … rabble … *to get their votes*! Hang them! It's pathetic!"

The snake slithered on, even slower now as it passed the junctions that led to commuterland. Somewhere up ahead there must have been an accident. Some life or other had melded with metal and would not be seeing the dawn come up on Saturday morning. He hated them for it, hated the fact that their lives—and their deaths—influenced his. He almost snarled as his thoughts returned to his situation.

Garden leave. Six months of skulking around the house. The odd trip to town to have lunch with someone trying to find out what was going on. His mood darkened as he thought of what would inevitably happen when he got home. Pulling up at his house, a small cottage set back behind a stand of trees, he would wind the window down and listen to the silence, as he always did on his return. A silence that welcomed no one, a silence that was his alone. Only the sound of the car's engine cooling, metal parts shrinking back into themselves.

He would undoubtedly argue with Philomena, his wife.

"I'd rather have ten years' garden leave than play their games," he would say, his voice rising. "This is me, Philomena. Do you want me to be someone else, to be false to my very nature?"

"I'd rather you had given it a go before you blew it completely!" she would reply, soft eyes flashing, slamming down the bottle of wine from which she had been pouring a glass. "Can't you … I don't know … go back and apologize? Tell them that stress got the better of you, or, or … something…?"

"Don't be stupid!" The familiar contempt would strangulate his words. He would be choking on it. He would stride from the room, the door slamming behind him, dislodging a horse brass from its place on the whitewashed wall.

As he approached the junction at which he would slough off the snake of cars, he had arrived at an understanding of the future. He knew he would have to drag himself away from the past, he would work with others to destroy what he had created, because that is what you did. Loyalty in business was no more than the raising or lowering of a finger and the world was no more than a road of slippery turns. Friends would become enemies. People he trusted would be out to defeat him in whatever he did.

Later he would sit, empty and soulless, nursing a generous helping of single malt, as the hours exchanged their meanings with each other, and the silence took on the colours of night. A world elsewhere … but where?

The Art of Persuasion

David Varela on *Richard III*

Principal Actor: John Rice

Some products sell themselves. One look at an iPod has been enough to persuade millions of people to part with their cash. A new Ferrari will always find a buyer. Superior style, unrivalled performance, excellent value, a reputation for quality—any of these will make the job of an ad exec so much easier.

But what if you're trying to sell a much tougher proposition? What if your product isn't, in fact, much cop at all? What if it's ugly, damaged, morally bankrupt and reviled by the public? And what if your target audience has already had a particularly bad experience with it?

Most ad agencies (if they even took on the job) would recommend starting from scratch—perhaps redesigning the product, rebranding it, and building a steady campaign to improve its reputation. The process would take a lot of hard work and rather a long time, but eventually, the market might be persuaded to buy it.

Anyone who claimed they could turn the situation round any quicker would be either a liar or a genius. Or, more likely, both.

Think different

Richard of York has something of an image problem these days. He certainly wasn't popular when *Richard III* was first performed, but Shakespeare's play has made matters worse in some respects, exaggerating Richard's physical deformities and making his vices seem blacker than they ever were in reality. Indeed, historians have argued that Richard's brief reign—just two years—was characterized by perfectly reasonable decisions that any king might have made. The murder of the princes in the Tower was a justifiable political move. They threatened the nation's stability. The fact that they were children added to the pathos, but didn't lessen the threat that they posed. I expect that modern governments have made similar unpalatable decisions.

But while Shakespeare did a certain amount of damage to Richard's legacy, he also enhanced aspects of his reputation. Richard is now regarded as a master of propaganda; which, given his brief reign and violent death, must be something of an amplification. In *Richard III*, the Duke of York not only benefits from having Shakespeare's eloquent tongue in his head, but also from a showy bias: in this play, Shakespeare delights in defending the indefensible, sending Richard into impossible debates and making sure he comes out victorious. He gives him a serpentine ability to make anyone believe anything. It may not be pretty, but it's a useful skill. I'm sure many ad execs would cheerfully bump off a few kids to acquire it.

Impossible is nothing

Shakespeare wants to demonstrate Richard's abilities right at the start of the story, so in just the second scene of the play, he sets him an insurmountable challenge. Richard declares that he will woo and marry the young, attractive Queen Anne. Never mind the fact that he killed her husband. Never mind that he also killed her father-in-law, who is being buried today. Never mind that Anne knows all about his crimes and hates him with a violent fury. And never mind that Richard looks like half a pantomime camel. He promises the audience that he will make Anne agree to be his wife, and the audience is intrigued by his confidence. How will he pitch this ugly proposal?

What follows is a masterclass in persuasion. It's worth taking a closer look at the scene, to see the strategies Richard uses to turn around this impossible client.

Because you're worth it

Anne makes her stance very clear. In a 30-line monologue, she explains just how much she hates the murderous Richard and goes into great detail regarding the horrors she wishes will befall him (and any future wife he might have). She is a firebrand of righteous anger. Into this strides the man himself: fearless, unshakably confident, tactless and aggressive. He demands that the pallbearers put down the corpse of Henry VI—whom he murdered—and let him talk to the grieving queen. One might expect a man in Richard's position to show remorse, to tread softly as he tries to woo the young widow, but no. He disrupts the funeral march, almost starts a fight with the guards, and shows no respect for the deceased. It's a bold move.

The audience has no idea how this approach is going to help Richard's cause. He's gone out of his way to offend the very person he wants to charm. So what's his plan?

Flattery. Richard has spotted that Anne has a weakness: her pride in her appearance and in her moral rectitude. For all her sermons and claims to virtue—and she's certainly more virtuous than Richard will ever be—she's vain. He focuses his assault entirely on that one small flaw.

When she gives him a mouthful for barging into the funeral, Richard apparently appeals to her better nature: "Sweet saint, for charity be not so curst." And when she continues her invective, he again asks for forgiveness, saying that she should be able to forgive anything, as she's so angelic. Naturally, this only makes her angrier.

At this point, he moves the argument on, offering to explain what happened. Anne (and the audience) are expecting him to blame someone else, to plead innocence, to come up with an alibi of some kind. But again, Richard takes a different tack.

Anne: *Didst thou not kill this King?*
Richard: *I grant ye, yea.*

He admits guilt in the murders of both men, showing an astonishing level of gall. How's he going to rescue the situation from here?

This is all, of course, part of Richard's plan. He's been leading Anne toward the crux of his argument:

Richard: *Is not the causer of the timeless deaths …*
As blameful as the executioner?
… Your beauty was the cause of that effect:
Your beauty, that did haunt me in my sleep
To undertake the death of all the world,
So I might live one hour in your sweet bosom.

So it was her fault. He killed her husband and the king because of her enchanting beauty. She is as much to blame as he is.

Anne's response is outwardly brave, but betrays a first sign of weakness:

Anne: *If I thought that, I tell thee, homicide,*
These nails would rend that beauty from my cheeks.

Valiant, hollow, words. Richard has taken a calculated risk, guessing that Anne is more likely to preserve her vain beauty than to safeguard her probity. The "If …" suggests that she's in two minds now. Richard has struck a nerve.

He presses on, confessing his devotion, and claiming he would be a much better husband than the old one and that this will all turn out for the best. Anne isn't fully convinced, so Richard moves into the next phase of the argument: the tearjerker.

He tells Anne that her beauty has made him weep— he, who has never wept despite all the trying circumstances he has faced … and he takes this opportunity to remind Anne, off-hand, about his own suffering. Admittedly, he lays it on a bit thick:

Richard: *These eyes, which never shed remorseful tear,*
No, when my father York and Edward wept
To hear the piteous moan that Rutland made …
Nor when thy warlike father, like a child
Told the sad story of my father's death,
And twenty times made pause to sob and weep,
That all the standers-by had wet their cheeks
Like trees bedash'd with rain. In that sad time
My manly eyes did scorn an humble tear …

Not only has he suffered terribly, but he has also proved himself to be more "manly" than even Anne's father, again hinting that he would be a superior substitute for the previous men in her life.

This pitiful monologue goes on for 20 lines, and Anne's silence is notable. She's thinking. Rethinking. Richard has softened her up and now he feels safe to push her for a decision, to close the deal.

Just do it

The method he chooses is risky, but again, he has a firm grip on the odds. He draws his sword with a melodramatic flourish, hands it to her and tells her to kill him or love him. Here, he mimics the struggle playing out in her mind:

Richard: *Nay, do not pause, for I did kill King Henry—*
But 'twas thy beauty that provoked me.
Nay, now dispatch: 'twas I that stabb'd young Edward—
But 'twas thy heavenly face that set me on.
[She falls the sword.]

Richard has always known that she isn't the murderous type, so this tightrope walk does have something of a safety net. However, he almost seems to be teasing her, daring her, recklessly putting his life in her hands. When she lets the sword drop, she concedes defeat. Seeing this, Richard hits her with a wonderful false opposition: "Take up the sword again, or take up me."

Anne, disoriented by the rhetoric, doesn't know what to believe anymore. Her firm convictions from the start of the scene have crumbled. Just minutes before, she had been sure that Richard was evil to the core. Now, she murmurs, "I would I knew thy heart." She has tacitly accepted the idea that, yes, her beauty could quite understandably drive a man to murder; and yes, she rather likes the idea of a strong, lethal protector who worships her heavenly face.

Richard offers her a ring, as a token, and she takes it. The deal is done.

What's most enjoyable is Anne's post-rationalization of her decision:

Anne: *With all my heart, and much it joys me too,*
To see you are become so penitent.

... not that Richard has shown the least bit of remorse. Through confidence, flattery and calls for sympathy he has appealed to the saint's vanity and achieved the unimaginable.

Pure genius

During this scene, there are two levels of persuasion. Richard is seducing Anne, but at the same time Shakespeare is seducing his audience. He's making them warm to his leading character—at the time, one of the nation's least loved historical figures. This is essential to the play's success. Entertainment depends on a degree of persuasion, and Shakespeare uses some subtle techniques to help make Richard an admirable anti-hero.

First, he allows Richard to address the audience. He takes us all into his confidence, making us complicit in his plans. Second, Shakespeare makes the challenge of seducing Anne as challenging as possible. He puts King Henry's corpse right there, on stage, as they argue over his dead body. He also makes Richard seem wholly responsible for the murder of Anne's husband, though actually he was just one of three conspirators. He refers to King Henry as Anne's "father," though actually he was only her father-in-law. And he gives Anne that long monologue at the start of the scene, allowing her to emphasize just how unthinkable a union with Richard would be. By making his position so difficult, Shakespeare makes Richard's victory seem all the more remarkable.

Richard's utter bamboozling of Anne displays a great deal of ingenuity—a vital quality in any protagonist. Nothing appeals to an audience more than a character who accepts a challenge and, through intelligence and skill, manages to defy the odds. In his own way, Richard is heroic. No one else can match him, and when he is finally defeated at Bosworth, there's a sense that he has been beaten by supernatural forces. No man, not even Henry Tudor, could conquer him unaided.

Have it your way

So how can any of these lessons be applied to your twenty-first-century writing? The main principle is to *make a virtue out of vice*—in your own position, but also in your audience's. For example, if your product or service has a bad reputation, be up front about it (especially if it's irrefutable). Admit to its weaknesses. List any prior misdemeanours. At least your honesty will be appreciated. And if your audience has any minor foibles—a lust for shiny things, a desire to brag, a belief that they're worth it, a willingness to nudge their fellow man out of the way—appeal to those too.

But while appealing to their vices, you mustn't make your audience feel guilty or sordid. Give them a way of justifying their decision. A large part of this is flattery. Instead of making someone feel cheap for choosing your economy product, praise their wisdom for being so thrifty. If you're selling a luxury product, compliment them on their impeccable taste.

You should also bear in mind that beauty isn't everything. Sex certainly sells some products, but when it comes to reliability or hard-nosed efficiency, earthiness can be a winner. How else can one explain the success of Cillit Bang's strident TV salesman, Barry Scott? If your product can't be sexy, make the most of its down-and-dirty ability to get things done. Make beauty seem a superficial mask that disguises weakness, while ugliness is an unvarnished display of honesty and effectiveness.

If you can (and this is the hardest part), be inventive. Show ingenuity in your approach. When one tactic is expected, try the opposite.

But in all these things, be *confident*. Think of the way Richard storms into that funeral, the way he lists his worst sins with a sword pointed at his heart. Take chances and dare to be called on them.

This may all sound rather mercenary. The manipulative Richard of York should not be the ideal role model for the modern businessman. But what's the difference between "manipulating an audience" and "taking them on a journey"? Choose your own metaphor. Essentially, it's a process of persuasion.

Every time we write, we're trying to persuade people—

to agree with our feelings, to like us more, or just to keep turning the page. Shakespeare knew how to give people what they wanted, and by understanding his audience's baser instincts, he created some of the most gripping, moving, enduring work in the literary world. Millions of people have been carried away by his verbal displays. But Shakespeare's rhetoric can also have an impact outside the theatre. His audience was much the same as yours is today, from the groundlings in the pit to the lords in the rafters. Everyone's still human. Understand that, and you'll have the power to turn eyesores into iPods, flops into Ferraris, and to keep the crowd shelling out for more.

Over and Above

The Players' Finale: by Jim Davies

"Another pestilent, hare-brained scheme foisted upon us by the marketing department," said Will Kemp, testily adjusting his codpiece.

It hadn't been a good day. Dame Roberta Benfield, his regular Mistress Quickly, had contracted a severe dose of shingles and retired hurt, ungracefully. Her stand-in, though a trier, just didn't cut the mustard. Each of her numerous double-entendres was accompanied by a ridiculously overblown gesture. A grotesque grinding of the hips. Air-drawing the shape of a crude phallus. Wobbling her flabby D-cups like a pair of blubbery jellies. Why didn't she just bring on a blackboard and spell it out for the audience?

In today's matinee, she had actually taken it upon herself (totally undirected) to pat his paunch as she uttered the line "He hath put all my substance into that fat belly of his." Talk about laying it on with a trowel. Where'd she trained anyway? The Benny Hill School of Dance and Drama? They'd let anyone into the RSC these days. He'd have words with the director … if he could be prised away from sweet-talking those Japanese sponsors.

And now this.

All 26 of them had been chivvied into Bob Armin's changing room straight after the performance. Here we go, yet another pep talk, they'd thought. But it was nothing of the sort. A couple of the management big-wigs, Shakespeare and Condell, sardined their way into the heaving space, accompanied by a wiry-haired fellow wearing a tweed jacket two sizes too large for him, and a lean and hungry look.

The post-match hubbub eased to an expectant hush. Players in incongruous states of déshabillé, marooned somewhere between the seventeenth and twenty-first centuries (Nick Tooley in Ramones T-shirt with hose, Jo Taylor in pointy cone-shaped hat and Nikes) cast wary eyes toward the doorway. "This," announced commercial director Harry Condell, with a trill of pride, "is Augustine Phillips, one of the country's foremost modernist composers. I'm sure you're familiar with his symphony *Casement Pilgrimage pt 4*, which featured such sublime recordings of Amazonian tree rustling. He has a modest proposal for you, which I hope you'll all find as deliciously intoxicating as I do. Augustine … the floor is yours."

The tweed jacket shuffled forward, and in a series of short, sharp bursts, like a hesitant sheep reciting from a phone book, proceeded to outline his curious stratagem. It had come to him on a recent ideas-finding trip to the Sahara. As he fell into a troubled, sweat-soaked sleep in a small desert town called Maroosa, he'd been half woken by a minaret calling the faithful to prayer. Then another piped up, another, and yet another, creating layer upon layer of sound that drifted in on the heat.

The effect was like a dream, past the wit of man to say what dream it was. An elaborate, detailed vision of the town slowly built up in his semi-conscious mind, like a shadowy Ordnance Survey map charted by the haunting drone of the *muezzin*. And quite unaccountably, familiar echoes of Shakespeare were wafted there too, producing a mesmerizing sonic tapestry of gently floating words and worlds.

Burbage farted with feeling. "Pardon me," he said. "I've been holding that in since Act 1."

Augustine rubbed his pointy chin and continued. It was his ambition, he revealed, to recreate a similar magical "dreamsoundscape" for the good burghers of Stratford-upon-Avon. Only, as minarets were in short supply in these parts, he proposed to employ a small flotilla of hot-air balloons instead. The score, which relied heavily on the mating call of the Saharan sand frog, was all but completed. The Shakespearean voices were to be supplied by the most accomplished actors in the land.

"That's you reprobates by the way," said Condell, a thin smile gashing his smug visage.

Augustine coughed, sounding even more ovine than before. He went on to posit various fanciful theories about the complex interrelationships of sound, sleep, dreams and the subconscious, and how he firmly believed that on the morning of his arcane experiment, Stratford would be making its way to work, bright, bewitched and miraculously inspired. And with that, he'd disappeared from the company like a conscientious sprite at daybreak.

The room's hubbub bubbed once more, though a divisive atmosphere had begun to pervade our once-merry troupe. Kemp and William Eccleston, gnarled old stagers who'd seen it all before, spread their cynicism like poison ivy.

"He thinks too much—such men are dangerous," said Eccleston. "Besides, there's no way on earth I'm climbing into a picnic basket with ideas above its station. My words and thoughts remain below."

"Though it may be madness, there is method in it," chipped in dapper artistic director Will Shakespeare, picking a worrying stray hair from his lapel. "But even if you don't accept the fellow's ideas, it's still the stuff of great team building."

"Team building? Team building? A pox on your team building," said Kemp, and he was off on one of his extended soliloquies, a lunatic glint recalling his rapturously received Lear of some years previous. He started gently on team building, pointing out that every rehearsal and performance was an unbeatable exercise in knitting the group as tight as a witches' coven. Paint-balling, go-karting, karaoke, clay pigeon shooting and the rest didn't hold a candle to a lusty evening's romp through *Richard III*.

Warming to his theme, he got stuck into all the other corporate fads and stress-busting strategies management had imposed on his colleagues over the years—yoga, Pilates, aromatherapy, scalp massage, Alexander technique, and life coaching. "Who needs life coaching when you've got Shakespeare?" he asked, a small fleck of foam evolving on the side of his mouth. "All life is here—love and war, life and death, humility and arrogance, treachery and loyalty, bears and Bottoms ... even the odd bare bottom. And as for role playing, what the blazes do you think we do all day long?"

Kemp slunk back, too drained to notice his applause was on the tepid side of lukewarm. In the far corner, John Shanks and Alexandra Cook whispered like Roman conspirators. Still throbbing with the youthful passion that had come to its head during their celebrated pairing as Romeo and Juliet, they had other ideas entirely. To this golden couple, sex was all—their chance to join the Half Mile High Club had arrived, and they weren't about to let it fly by. By their reckoning, if they managed the beast with two backs twice over, they might even qualify for full Mile High membership.

It was dark, unruly and 4 AM out on the Welcombe Hills just outside Stratford. Obscure birds clamoured, and strange lamentings seemed to carry in the air. The amber lights of the ancient town twinkled nonchalantly, oblivious to the foul machinations unfolding on their brow.

From a pair of Land Rovers, three bearded, befleeced men pulled yard after yard of balloon silk, like a magician pulling endless coloured handkerchiefs from his sleeve. Just as they'd finished laying their cargo down under the cast of their headlights, a third 4x4, choc-full of bulky sound equipment, pulled up.

"Early start Dick," remarked the red fleece to the driver.

"Yep ... big job this," replied Dick, slamming the door. "Why don't you get going over there with those two?"

But as these honest men of toil saw to the task in hand, evil lurked unnoticed in some bushes nearby. "We haven't got all night," whispered Sam Gilburne, her white-light Maglite casting strange, droopy shadows over his drawn visage. "Now's your chance ... they're over there working on some other balloons. That's the one we want."

"All right, hold your horses. It's as dark as pitch. Can't see what the hell I'm doing." It was Will Sly, peering like a resolute mole into his black rucksack.

"That's because you spent so long drinking up the courage to come up here in the first place. If these things are done, then it's best that they're done quickly. Are you man or mouse? Or maybe you'd like me to do it for you."

"Is this a Swiss army knife I see before me? So I cut the rope on the left-hand side? Come on then, pass me that CD ... no, over here."

With that, Sly shot out of his shadowy bolt hole, crouching and crawling until he reached his mark. His nefarious task was completed in a trice, and he stole stealthily back to their hiding place.

"OK, I've done the deed. What was that? Did you hear a noise?"

"Just an owl … maybe a cricket."

"A cricket? You don't get crickets in Warwickshire. Now … how do we get out of here without getting caught?"

They'd hatched their cankerous plot immediately after the meeting, over fiery Bloody Marys at the Falstaff Café. Its germ had been planted earlier as Sly passed three winos dispensing gobs of Special Brew wisdom from a park bench in Bancroft Gardens.

"All right, Sly! Top of the bill, top of the bill I tell you," said the first, dribbling into his mangy beard.

"All right Sly! The stars are yours, take your cue," croaked the second, before coughing up a wad of rubbery sputum.

"All right Sly! You shall rule the company hereafter," wheezed the third, wondering quite how to top his companions' repulsive discharge.

Sly quickly assumed his actorly composure. Swishing his luxuriant locks with the artfulness of a shampoo ad, he strode purposefully past the three scraggy stooges, his aquiline nose slanted at a distinctly upright angle. But they'd struck a nerve. How much longer was he to stand in the ample shadows of those pumped-up has-beens Kemp and Eccleston? He'd been leading man-in-waiting for an age, and his patience was at a low ebb.

His dashing Prince Hal and muscular Coriolanus were mere trifles. Fine, complex trifles, but trifles nevertheless. Now he intended to make history. To perform the greatest of all Danes and the most blood-curdling of Scottish thanes. To bestride the RSC stage like a colossus, staking his place among the pantheon of immortals, from Garrick and Kean, to Laughton and Olivier.

In his fierce, raven-haired lover Sam Gilburne, he had the perfect accomplice, ever-ready to stoke his vaulting ambition, and provide the oil for their axis of evil. If he faltered, she'd stand fast. If he turned, the blazing steel in her eye would prod him right back from whence he came. Will's coat tails were there for the riding. As sure as hell, she wasn't going to fall off.

Their plan was to strike right into their rivals' tenderest

spot. To inflict pain and humiliation so gruesome that Kemp and Eccleston would never quite recover. To annihilate their waning reputations, leaving them but the shells and husks of men.

"Ashes to ashes, hot air to hot air," said Sly, a coy smile flashing across his devilishly handsome features.

John Shanks and Alexandra Cook traversed the Welcombe Hills with a spring in their step, armed with a fresh supply of condoms for the bumpy flight ahead. When they arrived at the launch spot, they were most amused to find they'd been assigned a bright red balloon with the single word "Virgin" emblazoned on its side. Leaving nothing to chance, they'd spent the night apart to make sure their ardour was fully primed. But they needn't have worried. "Kiss me doll," sighed Shanks, and, seizing his pretty paramour to his gym-pumped breast, their hungry mouths locked once more into a savage tussle of tongues and tonsils.

The wind was as still as death. Apart from the odd forlorn twig that had been separated from its mother, there was little sign of the previous night's cataracts and hurricanoes. Like gaudy giants' pillowcases, seven wispy 100-foot-long nylon balloon bags lay spread flat along the grass, their garish corporate colours shocking the gentle green carpet beneath them. Pilots and technicians bustled around the equipment, busy stage-hands before the main performance, checking ropes and pulleys and burners and baskets, securing the sound equipment that would soon be sprinkling Augustine's sonic magic over the rooftops of Stratford.

Gradually, as if time had danced backward, various costumed players hove into view, their feathers and outsize hats preceding them as they cleared the crest of the hill in small clumps. Bob Armin arm in arm with Georgia Bryan; Nathan Field ploughing his own lonely furrow; Robert Gough with William Ostler; Tom Pope sharing a catholic joke with Jane Rice and Richard Robinson; John Underwood and Sam Crosse.

Kemp and Eccleston loitered at the back, muttering like a pair of disgruntled schoolboys forced to endure a cross-country run. They still couldn't figure quite how Shakespeare had persuaded them to take part in this farce. But then he had a way with words. His honey'd sentences had charmed them like the softest music to attending ears, until he'd convinced them that the whole enterprise depended on their presence.

A flaxen-haired man in a chunky red fleece ticked off the actors' names on a clipboard, and ushered them in the direction of their given craft. Augustine flapped about in a state of nervous anticipation, making a few final adjustments on his laptop, the digital baton that pulled the stings of his airborne orchestra. As the dragon roar of the propane burners rent the morning silence, the balloons swelled from flaccid sheaths to proud, upstanding monuments to Mammon.

"Damned if I'm going on that one," stage-whispered Kemp to Eccleston. It wasn't the innocuous royal blue colour he objected to so much as the 10-foot-high slogan reading "Tampax Mini—At Your Discretion." So, seizing their opportunity, the rotund pair breathlessly stole toward the only remaining unattended carriage. Decorated in a tasteful black with a cream top, this one bore the far more acceptable legend "Fly Goodness. Fly Guinness." "That's more like it," chuckled Eccleston. "And let's stop off for a couple afterwards." They were just in time. Augustine had already counted down, and like eager dogs released from their leads, the balloons careered heavenward.

At that moment, Will Sly and Sam Gilburne staggered into the light—gaunt, befuddled and with odd pieces of foliage caught in their hair. Their earlier efforts to escape undetected had been confounded. Confined to their bush, they'd eventually fallen into a troubled sleep, plagued by dark, gothic dreams and the sound of distant demonic laughter. And now, before they had the wherewithal to protest, the man in the red fleece had harried them on to the good ship Tampax. Suddenly and silently, they felt the ground dropping away from them, and watched hopelessly as the landscape below shrank into a mesmeric patchwork of greens and browns.

So it was that six balloons made their way in a tidy floating convoy toward the ancient town, drizzling their entrancing potpourri of Shakespeare's words and Augustine's notes over the gently waking citizens. The seventh, with its distinctive royal blue livery and neat plea for compact sanitary protection, was last seen veering out of control in the environs of Wolverhampton, squawking out "The Birdie Song."

On June 23 2006 at 6.30 AM, the residents of Stratford-upon-Avon were woken by seven hot-air balloons pumping out ambient music and readings from Shakespeare by actors Patrick Stewart and Janet Suzman. Composed by Dan Jones, the 45-minute performance was commissioned to celebrate the RSC's Complete Works Festival, and was also part of a university research study into how sound affects sleep.

Any similarity to actual facts and persons living or dead is coincidental and unintended.

Biographies

Rob Andrews' first introduction to Shakespeare was his dad reciting bits of rote-learned, never forgotten O-level text over Sunday lunch with *Jimmy Savile's Old Record Club* playing in the background. "Signior Antonio, many a time and oft/In the Rialto you have rated me/Now then. How's about that then, guys and gals." Now Rob is a Creative Director of R&D&Co.

Nick Asbury is a writer specializing in branding, literature and tone of voice work. He lives and works in London. Nick Asbury is also an actor, musician, fire-eater, fight scene choreographer, corporate voiceover artist and a member of the Royal Shakespeare Company. He lives and works in Stratford-upon-Avon.

John Bolton, City writer, has been helping businesses communicate better for ten years, but has always harboured more creative aspirations. Indeed, this book has been the ideal opportunity for John to sate his overweening ambition for literary respectability while still purporting to write about business. A Cambridge graduate and life-long lover of Shakespeare, John "guesses he likes the tragedies best."

Ezri Carlebach is Head of Internal Communications, UK Banking, for Barclays plc. Prior to that he worked in the voluntary sector for 18 years in various communication roles, most recently at the RSA, after a first career as a musician. Ezri serves on the UK board of the International Association of Business Communicators, and is a regular columnist for the *Journal of Employee Communication Management*.

Alastair Creamer is a musician by education, a painter by accident but a writer by necessity. During the day he helps others navigate between the worlds of art and business. He created and ran the Catalyst project at Unilever for seven years before leaving in 2006 to found his own company, creamer and lloyd, which works across business, the arts and education.

Nicola David is a freelance writer who, having spent her early career in IT, thinks she may have met Dilbert (although she insists she is not Tina the Tech Writer). She takes careful steps to conceal her own incompetence—especially from her clients, who include many high-profile retailers. She writes across a variety of formats, including editorial, online and print, and offers tone of voice consultancy.

Jim Davies is a commercial writer and design critic, and a founding director of 26. He is the author of *The Book of Guinness Advertising* and several books on design, and his distinctive brand of cultural commentary has appeared widely in international design magazines and national newspapers. Look out for his monthly column in *Design Week*.

Stuart Delves runs copywriting agency Henzteeth in Edinburgh. Coincidentally, Stuart's award-winning play *The Real Lady Macbeth* was revived in 2006 by the Brussels Shakespeare Society and won the FEATS Competition in Luxembourg before playing at the Actors' Church in Covent Garden and at the Complete Works Festival in Stratford. "Northern Light," an essay on George Mackay Brown and Orkney, appears in *Common Ground*.

Jack Elliott was a professional theatre and TV actor for many years before becoming a scriptwriter. He played Ferdinand in a very forgettable production of *The Tempest* in Belfast and adapted the play for a car launch in Bermuda. He now works primarily as a scriptwriter and teacher of writing skills.

Laura Forman, after almost five years as a writer at Interbrand, moved on to become the copy manager at John

Lewis in 2005. Her poems have featured in various magazines and, most recently, *Generation Txt*, an anthology of six twentysomethings published by *penned in the margins*. They're going on tour in 2007, so look out for a reading near you.

Mark Griffiths is one half of a husband and wife team of wordsmiths, consultants and hopeful idealists who wake up every morning in the shadow of Shakespeare. Specializing in brand language and corporate responsibility communications, Ideal Word helps brands, companies and organizations shape and communicate their image, ideas and ideals.

Lu Hersey, based in Bristol, has been an editor and copywriter for many years. One day she hopes to break free and release her inner Shakespeare.

Liz Holt has won 23 national and international creative awards for her advertising copy. She writes articles about copywriting and serves on awards judging panels in London and New York. Following years as a Head of Copy and Creative Director, she now works freelance. *Stolen Dreams*, her first novel, is set in the sixteenth century. Liz also writes children's stories.

Roger Horberry is a musician, copywriter and content strategist, whatever one of those is. His interest in Shakespeare's neologisms comes from a deep love of language. His interest in *King Lear* comes from a deep love of corpse-strewn endings.

Jamie Jauncey is a novelist, musician and business writer who lives in the centre of what was once Birnam Wood, which is doubtless why he was given *Romeo and Juliet*. Jamie is a director of the Edinburgh International Book Festival, the world's largest literary festival. His novel *The Witness* is published by Picador in summer 2007.

Gordon Kerr has been a freelance writer, editor, poet, journalist, brand consultant and grape picker. He has run marketing at Waterstone's and Bloomsbury but now markets the Danish furniture retailer ILVA and is editor of the

Poetry Writers' Yearbook. His children's book *The Time Traveller's Guide to Georgian London* is published in 2007.

Emma Lawson is a writer, editor and project manager. She's gone from books to magazines to websites to The Writer, and has been grateful for several enjoyable creative partnerships along the way.

Elen Lewis is a freelance writer. The former editor of *Brand Strategy*, she now writes for magazines and newspapers including *The Financial Times*. Elen's first book, *Great IKEA*, was listed in the top five business books of the year by *The Times* in 2005. Her second book, *Great Brand Stories: eBay*, was published in November 2006. Elen read English Literature at Oxford University.

Robert Mighall is the author of *A Geography of Victorian Gothic Fiction* (Oxford University Press, 1999), written while a lecturer at Oxford University. He is now a part-time consultant at design and branding agency, Lloyd Northover, and is currently writing a book about our relationship with sunshine. *Sunshine: A Love Affair* will be published by John Murray in spring 2008. Robert contributed a chapter on Dickens' *Great Expectations* for the 26 project *Common Ground*.

Brian Millar is Creative Director of Brandtacticians.com. He was previously an advertising copywriter and Creative Director at agencies including Saatchi & Saatchi and Ogilvy in New York, Paris and London. His work for IBM was voted one of the top ten campaigns of the decade in *Advertising Age* magazine. He currently works with clients including Pfizer, Reuters, Unilever, the South Bank Centre and the British Museum.

Andy Milligan is a business consultant and the author of three business books *Brand it Like Beckham*, *See Feel, Think, Do* and *Uncommon Practice*. He runs his own consultancy, Ambrand, and is a founding partner of Caffeine. He read English at Oxford University, where his entrance paper was on the theme of kingship in Shakespeare's history plays.

Katherine Peñaloza first encountered Shakespeare at age 14. It was her induction into the English language, and continues to inspire her own work—writing and consulting on branding issues in Asia. Katherine was Strategy Director at Interbrand Singapore. Recently, she took a break from client development work at McKinsey & Co to complete her first book on Singapore Airlines' branding.

Dan Radley roams the fields of graphic design, advertising, moving image and interactive media, thinking up ideas. His greatest enemy is his own brain and he spends most of his time trying to catch it by surprise. Dan currently works for brand design and digital agency Start, where he leads a team of writers.

Lin Sagovsky believes business people value performance, but don't do much rehearsal. As an actor and playwright, she helps redress that balance. Her consultancy, Play4Real (www.play4real.co.uk) creates and runs interactive plays, interpersonal skills workshops, private coaching in confident speaking, and strategic creativity programmes—for global corporates, government departments, SMEs, anywhere that business people want serious professionalism, new skills, unexpected answers—and sheer fun.

John Simmons is director of training and brand language at The Writer (www.thewriter.co.uk) where he runs workshops inspiring people to write more creatively for business. A former director of Interbrand, he currently works with Diageo, Espa, Unilever and 3. As editor of *Great Brand Stories*, published by Cyan, he has commissioned and written many books on brands including his latest on Innocent Drinks.

Fraser Southey is an independent writer and creative director with a background in advertising and design. He uses words and has ideas for a wide range of clients, including global corporations and creative services agencies. He enjoys writing, whatever the subject or medium. He lives in south-east London with his wife and three daughters and is a life-long Chelsea supporter.

Elise Valmorbida grew up Italian in Melbourne, Australia, but fell in love with London. Her first novel *Matilde Waltzing* (Allen & Unwin, Australasia) was nominated for two national literary awards. Her latest work, *The Book of Happy Endings* (Cyan Books, UK), is a collection of unusual short stories about love. Elise runs a communications consultancy and teaches creative writing at the University of the Arts London.

David Varela is a hybrid. Dividing his time between freelance projects and writing plays, he's seen as much drama in the office as he has on the stage. His work has appeared on BBC Radio 4, BBC7, ITV and at the Royal Court, the Hampstead Theatre and the National Theatre Studio. He also writes the alternate reality game Perplex City.

Rob Williams is Creative Director at Penguin Books. Since 2003 he has been involved with many of 26's projects and the accompanying books, including *26 Letters*, *From Here to Here* and as a contributing editor to *Common Ground*.

Shakespeare's Globe
21 New Globe Walk
London SE1 9DT
T: +44 (0)20 7902 1400

Performance

The Globe Theatre is a faithful reconstruction of the open-air playhouse designed in 1599, where Shakespeare worked and for which he wrote many of his greatest plays. The theatre season runs from May to October with productions of the work of Shakespeare, his contemporaries and modern playwrights.

Education and events

The Globe's acclaimed education programme is led by theatre practitioners who share their practical experience of Shakespeare and the theatre. From October to March all students enjoy exclusive access to the Globe stage. In addition to lectures and practical workshops, Globe Education provides interactive distance-learning projects and an extensive programme of seasonal lectures, workshops and staged readings for the general public.

Exhibition and theatre tours

Shakespeare's Globe Exhibition is the world's largest exhibition devoted to Shakespeare, his theatre and the London in which he lived and worked. A visit to the exhibition includes a lively and informative guided tour of the reconstructed theatre.

Friends and support

The Friends of Shakespeare's Globe enjoy a range of benefits including priority booking for the Globe Theatre season, *Around the Globe* magazine, free entry to Shakespeare's Globe Exhibition and discounts on Globe Education events. The Friends also fund a number of projects at Shakespeare's Globe, which receives no annual government subsidy. The support of the general public is vital to enable the Globe to grow and flourish.

To find out more, visit www.shakespeares-globe.org

OTHER TITLES BY 26

26 Letters: Illuminating the alphabet
Edited by Freda Sack, John Simmons and Tim Rich
(Cyan Books, 2004)

26 Malts: Some joy ride
Edited by Stuart Delves, Jamie Jauncey and Damian Mullan
(Cyan Books, 2005)

From Here to Here: Stories inspired by London's Circle Line
Edited by John Simmons, Neil Taylor, Tim Rich and Tom Lynham
(Cyan Books, 2005)

Common Ground: Around Britain in 30 writers
Edited by John Simmons, Rob Williams and Tim Rich
(Cyan Books/Marshall Cavendish Editions, 2006)

CYAN

26 Letters

Illuminating the Alphabet

Edited by Freda Sack, John Simmons and Tim Rich

CYAN

TWENTYSIX ORDINARY LABEL DESIGNS

26 MALTS

SOME JOY RIDE

EDITED BY STUART DELVES,
JAMIE JAUNCEY & DAMIAN MULLAN